SIGN

Michael A

CW00386341

IAN ALLAN
Publishing

CONTENTS

First published 1997

ISBN 0 7110 2518 5

© Michael A. Vanns 1997
Tabulation in Chapter 6 © Peter Kay and Roger Newman

Published by Ian Allan Publishing

an imprint of Ian Allan Ltd, Terminal House, Station Approach, Shepperton, Surrey TW17 8AS.
Printed by Ian Allan Printing Ltd at its works at Coombelands in Runnymede, England

Code: 9705/C2

Front cover:
The former GNR signalbox at Havenhouse on 4 October 1986. *Author*

Back cover:
Arnside, ex-Furness Railway, on 26 May 1996. *Author*

Title page (1):
On 6 April 1968, 4-6-0 No 45045 struggles past Cheadle Junction, an example of the CLC's first standard design of signalbox built from the 1870s until the first years of the 20th century. *R. Eldon*

Below (2):
Preserved Pacific No 71000 *Duke of Gloucester* powers past Abergele signalbox built in 1902 by the LNWR on its North Wales route between Chester and Holyhead. *John Shuttleworth*

Left (3):
Netley — an example of the L&SWR's first standard signalbox of the 1870s, photographed in 1909. *A. Sedgwick*

Below (4):
Oxspring Junction on the MS&LR's Woodhead route. An unusual signalbox with elements of the company's Type 2 & 3 designs of the 1880s. The box closed on 20 May 1973. *Robert Humm Collection*

ACKNOWLEDGEMENTS

The detailed facts and figures in this book come from much hard work on the part of many members of the Signalling Record Society over many years, and to them, and especially Peter Kay and Roger Newman, I am indebted. I would also like to thank Peter Waller, David Houlston, Peter Muxlow, John Powell, the Rev I. Ross of The Abbey, Shrewsbury, and the car salesman in Wigan who allowed me to climb on his showroom roof to photograph Wigan Wallgate signalbox.

BR(ER)	British Rail, Eastern Region
BR(LMR)	British Rail, London Midland Region
BR(NER)	British Rail, North Eastern Region
BR(ScR)	British Rail, Scottish Region
BR(SR)	British Rail, Southern Region
BR(WR)	British Rail, Western Region
C&H	Chester & Holyhead Railway
CLC	Cheshire Lines Committee
CR	Caledonian Railway
FR	Furness Railway
G&SWR	Glasgow & South Western Railway
GCR	Great Central Railway
GER	Great Eastern Railway
GNoSR	Great North of Scotland Railway
GNR	Great Northern Railway
GWR	Great Western Railway
HR	Highland Railway
L&YR	Lancashire & Yorkshire Railway
LB&SCR	London, Brighton & South Coast Railway
LC&DR	London, Chatham & Dover Railway
LMSR	London Midland & Scottish Railway
LNER	London & North Eastern Railway
LNW&GWJt	London & North Western & Great Western Joint Railway
LNWR	London & North Western Railway
L&SWR	London & South Western Railway
LT&SR	London, Tilbury & Southend Railway
M&CR	Maryport & Carlisle Railway
M&GNR	Midland & Great Northern Joint Railway
MR	Midland Railway
MS&LR	Manchester, Sheffield & Lincolnshire Railway
NBR	North British Railway
NER	North Eastern Railway
NLR	North London Railway
NSR	North Staffordshire Railway
SE&CR	South Eastern & Chatham Railway
SER	South Eastern Railway
SR	Southern Railway
TVR	Taff Vale Railway

An Ian Allan *abc* guide to signalboxes is long overdue. In many ways it is almost too late. If the book had appeared when the first locomotive *abc* was published during World War 2, there would probably have been almost 10,000 signalboxes to see all over the country. Today there are just under a thousand left on the national network, ie what used to be British Rail.

Signalboxes were taken for granted until comparatively recently. Then, as with any endangered species, systematic study and classification came when extinction was thought to be a real possibility.

It was during the 1950s that people began to take a real interest in our railway infrastructure — station buildings, goods sheds and signalboxes — rather than just the locomotives. Station buildings were perhaps already an acceptable subject to be interested in because they were considered not far removed from mainstream architecture. But signalboxes were perceived as part of an industrial legacy and that was not a recognised area for study until the 1960s. Interest grew as the abolition of signalboxes accelerated, firstly due to the implementation of the 1955 Modernisation Plan, and then with the closure of lines following the 1963 Beeching Report. In 1969 a group of signalling enthusiasts got together to form the Signalling Record Society, one of its aims being, as its title implied, to record surviving signalboxes and operating procedures.

Published information about signalling until then had tended to concentrate on equipment and procedures, ignoring the architectural aspects and different styles of signalboxes. In periodicals, photographs of signalboxes without engines or trains present were unusual. During the 1970s, however, publications began to appear which examined signalboxes from an architectural perspective as well as an operational one. In 1972 the first serious study of an individual post-Grouping company's signalling was

Above (5):
The remains of a Saxby & Farmer frame dumped at Clare, on the ex-GER Stour Valley line, photographed in February 1967. The passenger service through Clare ended that year. *P. Hocquard*

published by OPC — *A Pictorial Record of LMS Signals* by L. G. Warburton and V. R. Anderson. This was followed a year later by a more comprehensive volume — *A Pictorial Record of Great Western Signalling* by Adrian Vaughan, which in many ways set the standard for future books on signalling. In 1976 a little booklet compiled by M. A. King illustrating the variety of surviving signalboxes was published by Turntable Publications, and by 1983, there was a book covering the signalling and signalbox styles of every post-Grouping company, including their pre-Grouping constituents. The only published work concentrating solely on one pre-Grouping company is Richard D. Foster's impressive *Pictorial Record of LNWR Signalling*, published in 1982.

Since the formation of the Signalling Record Society, individual members had been meticulously researching, listing and classifying signalbox styles. Over the years the fruits of that work appeared in the Society's newsletter, but the average railway enthusiast was unaware of all this patient hard work until 1986 when OPC published *The Signal Box*. To date it remains the most comprehensive work on the subject.

Other booklets followed on specialist signalling subjects written by SRS members, the most relevant to this book being *Signal Box Directory*, published by Peter Kay in 1987. The lists of signalboxes currently surviving on the national network which appear in this book are based on his work and the author is most grateful to him for allowing his work and that of colleagues to be used here. The lists contain only a small proportion of the detail in the latest Directory, and readers interested in lever frame types, signalboxes in Ireland, on the London Underground and in preservation, and a host of other minutiae should obtain *Signalling Atlas & Signal Box Directory Great Britain & Ireland* published by Peter Kay,

Flat 2, Orchard House, Orchard Gardens, Teignmouth, South Devon, TQ14 8DP.

It is important to remember that signalboxes, powerboxes and signalling centres cannot be visited without prior arrangements being made with the various Railtrack zones. Permission to visit will rarely be given.

Below right (6):
Exeter City Basin (Type BR(WR)37a), an example of a late design of mechanical signalbox, opened on 9 December 1962 and closed on 17 November 1986. *Author*

Below (7):
The remains of the signalbox at Glamis on the CR's main line north of Dundee, photographed in May 1993. *Author*

DEFINITION OF A SIGNALBOX

It is appropriate at the outset to define what is meant by a signalbox. Here is the current author's definition: a building containing equipment to alter and control route setting and aspects of fixed signals to be observed and responded to by train drivers, and the means to communicate between other buildings so equipped, and with train drivers, to co-ordinate the movements of trains along sections of line.

*1. FIRST GENERATION OF
SIGNALBOXES 1850-1870*

If we use the above definition of a signalbox, then such buildings did not appear until the 1860s. During the previous decade, all the elements that in combination were to create signalboxes, evolved separately. This is a very interesting period which would repay further study. There was both marked individuality and surprising standardisation between companies. Photographs are few and it is all too easy to assume that certain developments were unusual or typical, when in fact they were not.

In the early years of the 1850s, fixed signals (both semaphore and other shaped boards) were the accepted means of stopping and starting trains. Trains were dispatched between stations using the 'time interval' system, and apart from at tunnels, signalmen at adjacent stations were unable to communicate with each other to ascertain whether the line was unobstructed for the passage of a train or not. Many stations were connected by the electric telegraph, but this was not initially used to regulate the movement of trains directly. Rather it was used in an indirect way, for example, to report delays that would need the running of other trains to be altered, or perhaps special requests for more carriages to be coupled to trains at stations. Telegraph instruments were invariably located in station buildings, whilst signalmen went about their work outside in all weathers.

As the decade progressed, signalmen were provided with huts just big enough to keep them protected from the elements. At some stations, raised platforms or towers were erected, so they could see further and had more time to react to approaching trains. Sometimes these structures also incorporated simple huts. At junctions it soon became usual to elevate the controlling semaphores on a platform along with the stirrups or levers to operate them and the points.

By the end of the 1850s, levers for operating signals and points were being grouped together, and various patents for

Below (8):
Brighton North signalbox of 1862, a heavily re-touched photograph from a Saxby & Farmer catalogue. *Transport Trust Library*

the means of controlling their operation led in 1860 to the appearance of the first recognisable frames of levers — or lever frames — with interlocking between every lever. These frames were not designed to be left outside like their predecessors, and so the elevated platforms and simple huts of the previous decade developed into glazed cabins. This logical step had been anticipated by John Saxby. In 1858, two years after the patenting of his 'Simultaneous Motion' mechanism, a drawing appeared showing it in such a cabin with the semaphores growing out of the roof. The design probably owed something to the mechanical telegraph towers of the south coast which also had semaphores or shutters growing out of the roofs. *(Picture 8)*

Saxby's cabins set the standard for the

Top (9):
Northfleet station showing on the left a typical SER signalman's hut of the 1860s with point lever in front. *Lens of Sutton*

Above (10):
An example of the first generation of SER signalbox developed from the signalman's huts. Catford Bridge, photographed in April 1969. *J. Scrace*

Opposite (11):
The signalbox built by the GNR in 1869 where its main line crossed the MR's Nottingham-Lincoln line at Newark. 'O2' No 63978 on an up freight, 23 May 1953. *J. P. Wilson*

look of many early signalboxes, but it is interesting to see (because photographs of early signalling installations survive) that on the SER that company's signalboxes developed in a slightly different way. Photographs show that SER huts by the 1860s incorporated one or two ordinary sash windows. *(Picture 9)* When the first signalboxes to contain lever frames appeared, they were simply scaled up versions of those huts, with multiples of the same ordinary sash windows. For many years SER boxes did not have continuous glazing along the front, but rows of individual sashes. *(Picture 10)*

The final element in the evolution of the signalbox was the introduction into the new cabins of the electrical instruments to enable signalmen to communicate between each other. During the 1850s, the principles of the 'block system' had been developed, whereby signalmen exchanged coded messages before allowing trains to pass between 'signal stations', and early in the following decade a number of instruments were patented to allow this system to be put into operation by any company willing to buy them. It was not until the beginning of the 1870s that the block system was adopted to any significant degree, but by then the signalbox had assumed the basic form that would characterise it for the next 100 years.

2. SECOND GENERATION
OF SIGNALBOXES 1870-1880s
The first obvious development that distinguished many boxes built at the end of the 1860s from those of the second generation was the alignment of the roofs. Those signalboxes which had evolved from huts, were often built with their gable ends parallel to the track. *(Picture 11)* The 1870s lever frames were longer than their predecessors of the 1860s, and it was realised by a number of railway companies that it was more convenient to accommodate larger lever frames in buildings with their gables at right angles to the track. This type of building was also easier to extend if a larger frame was needed at some later date.

Most of the first signalboxes derived from huts, as well as Saxby's first signalboxes had no architectural pretensions. Saxby's elevated signalboxes were basically signalling platforms with the addition of walls and glazing to protect the lever frame and later the block instruments. *(Picture 12)* They were simply functional buildings. It is noticeable in the second generation of boxes that the look of the structures became as important as their function. Put another way, signalboxes became respectable, those designing them

adding standard Victorian architectural details to reinforce this. Most brick-based signalboxes incorporated the sort of features you would find on many domestic buildings of the period — eg square brick chimneys, pitched tiled roofs, standard-sized doors and locking room windows. Some designers even reinforced the domestic feel by incorporating decorative barge-boards and finials that came straight from the 'cottage orné' and 'rustic' tradition of 1840s architecture. (Picture 13) Only the continuous glazing along the front branded signalboxes as a unique industrial building type.

The majority of signalboxes would never have been considered as architecturally

Above (12):
The purely functional Saxby signalbox at Lovers Walk on the LB&SCR, with its more self-conscious replacement to the left. *Bucknall Collection, Ian Allan Library*

Left (13):
The ex-GNR signalbox just north of Peterborough, photographed in June 1996. *Author*

Opposite top (14):
Park South, between Askam and Dalton on the FR, photographed in May 1996. *Author*

Opposite right (15):
The MS&LR signalbox at Stalybridge, photographed in July 1996. *Author*

significant. But the Furness Railway's Type 3 design of the 1880s were examples of signalboxes that came closest to being part of fashionable contemporary architecture. *(Picture 14)* With tapering bases built from beautifully dressed ashlar stone pierced by tall narrow locking room windows, and with hipped tiled roofs, they gave the impression of being part of medieval castles. In many ways they were close to the mediaevally inspired work of influential architects Anthony Salvin (1799-1881) and William Burges (1827-1881). The styles of signalboxes, however, cannot be attributed to individual designers, and they are credited only to the contractors who built them and the railway companies who operated them.

This decade, and into the next, proved a lucrative time for signalling contractors. Stevens & Sons of London had been supplying semaphores since the late 1840s, had developed one of the first effective fully interlocked lever frames in 1860, and were in an ideal position to profit from the sudden increased demand for signalling equipment

Top (16):
Saxby & Farmer's signalbox at East Grinstead (LB&SCR). Photographed on 19 August 1985, closed on 18 July 1987. *John Powell*

Above (17):
Tutbury Crossing, built for the NSR by McKenzie & Holland at the beginning of the 1870s. Photographed May 1996. *Author*

Opposite above (18):
Bromley Cross signalbox, built for the L&YR in 1875

to Yardley & Co's own design. Photographed June 1996. *Author*

Opposite centre (19):
West Thurrock Junction, built by the Railway Signal Co Ltd in 1892 for the LT&SR. Photographed in June 1965 and closed in April 1996. *Q. Neale*

Opposite bottom (20):
An example of a Railway Signal Co standard design built for the MS&LR in 1885. Photographed in November 1990. *Author*

Opposite above (21):
Parbold signalbox between Southport and Wigan photographed in June 1996. Built for the L&YR in 1877 to Saxby & Farmer's Type 9 design. *Author*

Opposite centre (22):
An example of a Saxby & Farmer's Type 5 signalbox built for the LB&SCR in 1884. Photographed in August 1986 and closed in July the following year. *John Powell*

Opposite below (23):
The standard McKenzie & Holland type of signalbox at Baschurch, December 1986. *John Powell*

Above (24):
Cowbridge Junction, TVR, the standard McKenzie & Holland design with added decoration for this particular Welsh company. *Author's Collection*

in the 1870s and 80s. *(Picture 15)* John Saxby joined forces with John Farmer supplying metal and timber signalling equipment and building distinctive signalboxes on many railways throughout the country. *(Picture 16)* McKenzie & Holland in Worcester also supplied equipment and fittings as well as its own design of signalbox, *(Picture 17)* as did Yardley & Co of Manchester, *(Picture 18)* and from 1881 the Railway Signal Co Ltd of Fazakerley, *(Pictures 19 & 20)* amongst others.

The styles of signalboxes manufactured by all these firms changed subtly throughout the period. Saxby & Farmer produced 11 recognisable types of box up to the end of the 1880s, many of them obviously tailored to the specifications of individual railway companies. *(Picture 21 & 22)* By comparison, McKenzie & Holland developed only three types in the space of about five years, Type 3, either completely timber or with a brick base, first appearing in the mid-1870s and staying in production until 1921. *(Picture 23)* The only significant modification to this style appears to have been for the TVR, which asked for decorative barge-boards and ridge tiles on its signalboxes. *(Picture 24)*

Not all signalling work was left completely in the hands of outside contractors, however. Often railway companies using their services would specify their own signalbox design. From the 1870s onwards, a number of railway companies developed distinctive styles which helped establish what we would call today their corporate identity. Inevitably, some of the first company designs were strongly influenced by the work of the early contractors, *(Pictures 25 & 26)* but successive modifications reinforced a definite house style. As each company's particular design evolved, it did more to unite their network of lines than perhaps any other structure. If

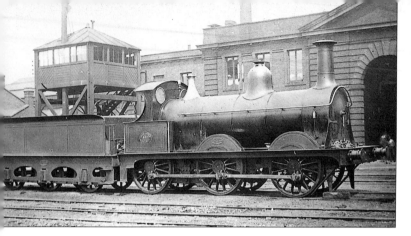

Above (25):
Outside the GER's Stratford locomotive works in the early 1870s, showing an elevated signalbox based very closely on Saxby's first design of the previous decade. *Bucknall Collection, Ian Allan Library*

Left (26):
Dorrington signalbox built by the LNW&GWJt Rly in the early 1870s to a design derived from early Saxby cabins. Photographed under BR supervision in December 1985. *Author*

Below left (27):
The MR Type 4a signalbox built on the Nottingham to Lincoln line at Newark in 1912. Photographed in June 1991. *Author*

Above (28):
Inside the impressive Crewe North Junction signalbox of 1906. Photographed in 1936 and closed during World War 2. *Real Photographs, E1078*

there was not a train in sight, then a signalbox would immediately betray the company's identity.

The MR was particularly successful in this respect; the majority of the features that first appeared in its early 1870s signalboxes were retained with only subtle alterations in subsequent new building until the company lost its separate identity in the Grouping of 1923. *(Picture 27)* There was no mistaking a MR signalbox. Even after Grouping, the new LMSR standard signalbox had recognisable MR features. The L&YR and the LNWR also maintained a consistent style over many years.

3. THIRD GENERATION
OF SIGNALBOXES 1890-1922
By the 1890s a number of railway companies were manufacturing their own signalling equipment and building their own signalboxes which were, on the whole, larger than their predecessors. Mechanical signalling was not only taken for granted, but the success of any new installation was judged by the complexity of track layout, the size of any new signalboxes, the number of their levers and the variety of semaphores and ground signals they operated. Big was beautiful and quantity seemed the mark of quality. In 1898 it was calculated there were 25,543 signalmen employed throughout the country, slightly more than there were engine drivers (22,237).

Only a decade later, however, this philosophy was being questioned. At major stations, hundreds of semaphore arms on massive gantries — each arm operated by its own lever in the signalbox — were no longer an acceptable solution. By the time the largest mechanical signalbox ever built, Locomotive Junction just south of York station on the NER, opened in June 1909 with 295 levers, a new generation of signalling engineers had already been experimenting with ways of reducing the size of signalboxes, not increasing them. For example, in 1899, the LNWR had installed an 'All-Electric Signalling' installation with miniature levers at Gresty Lane, Crewe, and in November 1906 successfully commissioned Crewe North Junction with 266 miniature levers. *(Picture 28)* Other companies were also experimenting, but despite the technological advances, all the new equipment was fitted into signalboxes that were indistinguishable from their mechanical counterparts. The outward appearance of new signalboxes did not alter significantly until after the 1920s. Companies did

17

introduce new designs, but all were firmly rooted in acceptable Victorian practice. The advances in equipment were not reflected in advances of signalbox design.

SIGNALLING CONTRACTORS' SIGNALBOX DESIGNS 1870-1922

The following is a list of surviving signalboxes on the national network organised by the contractors' type allocated to them by the Signalling Record Society and the date they were built. (This list [below] does not include preserved signalboxes.)

Type	Date	Signalbox
Dutton1 (Cambrian)	1891	Caersws
Dutton2 (McK&H)	1907	Pwllheli West Frame
EOD (SER)	1899	Maidstone West
GWCo (L&YR)	1879	Blackrod Junction
GWCo (L&YR)	1879	Chorley
McK&H1 (GWR)	1875	Henwick
McK&H1 (NSR)	1872	Tutbury Crossing
McK&H2 (GWR)	1876	Hartlebury
McK&H3/HR	c1890	Blair Atholl
McK&H3/HR	1890s	Clachnaharry
McK&H3/HR	1891	Nairn East
McK&H3/HR	1891	Nairn West
McK&H3/HR	1896	Forres East
McK&H3/HR	nk	Kingussie
McK&H3/HR	1898	Aviemore
McK&H3 (GWR)	1880	Baschurch
McK&H3 (GWR)	1880	Pontrilas
McK&H3 (GWR)	1883	Little Mill Junction
McK&H3 (GWR)	1884	Gobowen North
McK&H3 (GWR)	1885	Ledbury
McK&H3 (GWR)	1885	Park Junction
McK&H3 (Rhymney)	nk	Ystrad Mynach South
RSCo Hipped (GNoSR)	1888	Kennethmont
RSCo s/h	1894	Collyhurst Street
RSCo/West Highland Extension	1901	Mallaig
RSCo (L&YR)	1884	Halifax
RSCo (L&YR)	1884	Mill Lane Junction
RSCo (L&YR)	1888	Walkden
RSCo (L&YR)	1889	Philips Park No1
RSCo (L&YR)	1889	Philips Park No2
RSCo (L&YR)	1889	Rochdale
RSCo (L&YR)	1889	Salwick
RSCo (L&YR)	1890	Baguley Fold Junction
RSCo (L&YR)	1890	Miles Platting Junction
RSCo (LT&SR)	1894	Woodgrange Park
RSCo (MS&LR)	1885	Appleby (Lincs)
RSCo (MS&LR)	1885	Barrow Road Crossing
RSCo (MS&LR)	1885	Brigg
RSCo (MS&LR)	1885	Elsham
RSCo (MS&LR)	1886	Godnow Bridge

Type	Date	Signalbox
RSCo (MS&LR)	1886	Kirton Lime Sidings (Picture 29)
RSCo (MS&LR)	1886	Medge Hall
RSCo (MS&LR)	1886	Northorpe
S&F12a (SER)	1893	Sturry
S&F12a (SER)	1893	Wateringbury
S&F12a (SER)	1893	Wye
S&F12a (SER)	1894	Charlton Lane Crossing
S&F12a (SER)	1894	Robertsbridge
S&F12a (SER)	1894	Rye
S&F1b (LB&SCR)	c1876	Billingshurst
S&F5 (LB&SCR)	1876	Pevensey
S&F5 (LB&SCR)	c1876	Havant
S&F5 (LB&SCR)	1877	Holmwood
S&F5 (LB&SCR)	1877	Warnham
S&F5 (LB&SCR)	1878	Pulborough
S&F5 (LB&SCR)	1879	Berwick
S&F5 (LB&SCR)	1879	Newhaven Town
S&F5 (LB&SCR)	1882	Chichester
S&F5 (LB&SCR)	1882	Eastbourne
S&F5 (LB&SCR)	1883	Polegate Crossing
S&F5 (LB&SCR)	1886	Newhaven Harbour
S&F5 (LB&SCR)	1888	Lewes
S&F5 (LB&SCR)	1891	St Leonards West Marina
S&F (LBSCR)	1876	Bexhill
S&F6 (L&YR)	1873	Daisyfield Station
S&F6 (L&YR)	1873	Horrocksford Junction
S&F8 (L&YR)	1876	Brierfield Station (Picture 30)
S&F9 (L&YR)	1877	Parbold
S&F9 (L&YR)	1878	Towneley LCF
S&F9 (L&YR)	1879	Singleton
S&F (MS&LR)	1874	Shireoaks Station
Stevens n/s (CLC)	1886	Knutsford East
Stevens n/s (CLC)	nk	Northenden Junction
Stevens/MS&LR	1886	Stalybridge
Stevens (L&YR)	1874	Wooley Coal Siding
Stevens (SER)	1882	Grain Crossing
Yardley 1 (L&YR)	1875	Bromley Cross
Yardley 1 (L&YR)	1875	Hensall Station
Yardley 2 (L&YR)	1878	Milner Royd Junction

Dutton — Dutton & Co Ltd, Worcester

EOD — Evans, O'Donnell, Chippenham

GWCo — Gloucester Wagon Co

PRE-GROUPING RAILWAY COMPANY STYLES OF SIGNALBOX

The following is a list of surviving signalboxes on the national network organised by the railway company type allocated to them by the Signalling Record Society and the date they were built. (This list [right] does not include examples of designs built after Grouping, nor preserved signalboxes.)

Left (29):
Kirton Lime Sidings on the ex-MS&LR line between Gainsborough and Wrawby Junction, photographed in January 1989. *Author*

Below (30):
Brierfield Station signalbox (S&F8[L&YR]) just outside Burnley, photographed in June 1996. *Author*

Below right (31):
The distinctive ex-CLC signalbox at Mobberley, photographed in June 1996. The frame was replaced in July 1991 by switches on the block shelf. *Author*

Type	Date	Signalbox
Barry Rly		
Barry 1	1897	Barry
Barry 2	1897	Aberthaw
CLC		
CLC1a	1894	Mouldsworth Junction
CLC1b	1886	Mobberley *(Picture 31)*
CLC2	1908	Plumley West
CR		
Cal n/s	1870s	Cumbernauld
Cal n/s	1871	Larbert Junction
Cal n/s	1882	Carmuirs West Junction
Cal N1	1870s	Plean Junction
Cal N1	1873	Hilton Junction
Cal N1	1876	Carmont
Cal N1	1876	Newtonhill
Cal N1	u1874	Barnhill
Cal N1	1877	Craigo
Cal N1	1877	Errol
Cal N2	1891	Greenloaning
Cal N2	1892	Larbert North
Cal N2	1895	Auchterarder
Cal N2	1898	Carnoustie
Cal N2	1900	Stirling North
Cal N2	1901	Stirling Middle
Cal N2	1901	Stonehaven
Cal N2	1910	Laurencekirk
Cal N3	1902	Dunblane
Cal N3	1903	Gartsherrie South Junction

Above (32):
Drigg (FR) in May 1996. *Author*

Right (33):
Jumble Lane signalbox, protecting Kendray Street level crossing at Barnsley station in July 1996. Due to close in the summer of 1997. *Author*

Below right (34):
The ex-GER signalbox at Saxmundham, photographed in June 1996. Since February 1986 this box has supervised the RETB on the East Suffolk line between Westerfield (just outside Ipswich) & Oulton Broad North (just outside Lowestoft). *Author*

Type	Date	Signalbox
Cal N3	1905	Polmaise
Cal N3	1908	Fouldubs Junction
Cal S4	1894	Barrhead
Cal S4	1899	Gartcosh Junction
Cal S4	nk	Garnqueen North Junction
Cal S4	nk	Greenfoot
FR		
Furness 1	1874	Bootle
Furness 1	1874	Drigg *(Picture 32)*
Furness 2	1890	Askam
Furness 3	1883	Park South
Furness 3	1891	St Bees
Furness 4	1896	Carnforth F&M Junction
Furness 4	1898	Plumpton Junction
Furness 4	1900	Ulverston
Furness 4	1902	Dalton Junction
Furness 4	1903	Carnforth Station Junction
Furness 4	1907	Barrow-in-Furness
Furness 4	1918	Sellafield
Furness	nk	Arnside
Furness	1879/1909	Foxfield
Furness	1917	Millom
G&SWR		
GSW1	1876	Annan
GSW1	1877	Mauchline No1
GSW3	1893	Girvan
GSW3	1895	Kilkerran
GSW3	1897	Stranraer Harbour
GSW7	1905	Glenwhilly
GSW7	1909	New Cumnock
GSW7	1911	Kirkconnel
GSW7	nk	Holywood
GCR		
GC n/s	1910	Goxhill
GC n/s	nk	Beighton Station
GC n/s	nk	Jumble Lane *(Picture 33)*
GC5	1905	Brancliffe East Junction
GC5	1905	Dinting Station
GC5	1906	Ashburys
GC5	1906	Guide Bridge
GC5	1907	Dinnington Colliery
GC5	1908	Marsh Junction
GC5	1910	Ulceby Junction
GC5	1912	Immingham East Junction
GC5	1912	Immingham Reception Sidings
GC5	1912	Immingham West Junction
GC5	1912	Maltby Colliery South

Type	Date	Signalbox
GC5	1914	Barnetby East
GC5	1914	Brocklesby Junction
GC5	1914	Shireoaks East Junction
GC5	1915	Welbeck Colliery Junction
GC5	1916	Wrawby Junction
GC5	1917	Clipstone West Junction
GC5	nk	Kiveton Park Station
GER		
GE1/S&F	1876	Roydon
GE2	1877	Wymondham South Junction
GE2	1880	Kennett
GE2	1881	Downham
GE2	1881	King's Lynn Junction
GE2	1881	Saxmundham *(Picture 34)*
GE2	1881	Spooner Row
GE2	1881	Stowe
GE2	1882	Blotoft
GE2	1882	Gosberton
GE2	1882	Littleport
GE2	1882	Mill Green
GE2	1882	Sleaford North
GE2	1882	Thorpe-le-Soken
GE2/GN	1882	West Holmes
GE3	1882	Stowmarket
GE3/McK&H	1883	Manea *(Picture 35)*
GE3/S&F	1883	Acle
GE3/Stevens	1883	Brundall
GE4/McK&H	1883	Attleborough
GE4/McK&H	1883	Eccles Road
GE4/McK&H	1883	Harling Road
GE4/McK&H	1883	Shippea Hill
GE4/McK&H	1883	Thetford
GE4/S&F	1884	Yarmouth Vauxhall
GE4/S&F	1885	Lakenheath
GE4/Stevens	1883	Dullingham
GE5/S&F	1885	March East Junction
GE6	1885	Lowestoft *(Picture 36)*
GE7	1887	Cantley
GE7	1887	Whittlesea
GE7	1890s	Marks Tey
GE7	1891	Clacton
GE7	1891	Derby Road
GE7	1891	Trimley
GE7	1893	Forest Gate Junction
GE7	1894	South Tottenham
GE7	1896	North Walsham *(Picture 37)*
GE7	1898	Spelbrook
GE7	1899	Chelmsford
GE7	1900	Wroxham

Left (35):
Manea signalbox on the ex-GER line between March and Ely with its unique 'Dexion' steps. Photographed June 1996. *Author*

Below left (36):
Lowestoft signalbox photographed in June 1996. *Author*

Above right (37):
North Walsham signalbox, still a credit to the railways in Norfolk. Photographed in June 1996. *Author*

Left (38):
The GNR's last signalbox design, represented here by Spalding No 1, photographed in August 1996. *Author*

Type	Date	Signalbox
GE7	1901	Three Horse Shoes
GE7	1901	Oulton Broad North Junction
GE7	1904	Reedham Junction
GE7	1904	Reedham Swing Bridge
GE7	1904	Somerleyton Swing Bridge
GE7	1905	Enfield Town
GE7	1905	Ingatestone
GE7	1905	Seven Sisters Junction
GE7	1907	Oulton Broad Swing Bridge
GE7	1909	Whitlingham Junction
GE7	1912	Westerfield Junction
GE7	1920	Chingford
GE7/Dutton	1899	Kings Dyke
GE7/McH&H	1888	Bury St Edmunds Yard
GE7/McK&H	1887	St Margarets
GE7/McK&H	1888	Hertford East
GNR		
GN1	1872	Barnby Moor & Sutton
GN1	1874	West Station Junction (Boston)
GN1	1875	Allington Junction
GN1	1875	Littleworth
GN1	1875	Ranskill
GN1	1875	Bingham
GN1	1876	Bottesford West Junction
GN1	1876	St James Deeping
GN1	1876	St Nicholas Deeping
GN1	1877	Beckingham
GN1	1877	Finningley
GN1	1876	Heckington
GN1	1877	Stow Park
GN1	1878	Foxton
GN1	1880	Ancaster
GN1	1880	Grove Road
GN1	1880	Rauceby
GN1	1882	Barkston East Junction
GN1	1882	Sleaford East
GN1	u1874	Pelham Street Junction
GN1	1883	Skegness
GN1	1888	Thorpe Culvert
GN1	1888	Sibsey
GN1	u1877	Gainsborough Lea Road
GN1	1898	Helpston
GN1	1899	Wainfleet
GN1	nk	Eastfield
GN1	1874	High Street (Lincoln)
GN1	c1873	East Holmes
GN1	c1880	Sleaford West
GN3	1889	Rectory Junction
GN4a	1913	Bellwater Junction

Left (39):
St Mary's Crossing just outside Chalford on the GWR's 'Golden Valley' line. When this photograph was taken in May 1995 the former signalbox had long since ceased to control passing trains. *Author*

Below (40):
The ex-GWR signalbox at Moreton-in-Marsh, photographed in May 1988. *John Powell*

Bottom (41):
The L&SWR's signalbox at Petersfield photographed in December 1988. *Author*

Above (42):
An example of the L&SWR's late 19th century design of signalbox at Haslemere, photographed in November 1989. *Author*

Right (43):
An example of the brick-based standard L&YR design of signalbox derived from the Railway Signalling Co's pattern. Photographed in June 1996. *Author*

Below right (44):
The all-timber version of the L&YR standard signalbox at Barnsley that would have been prefabricated at Horwich Works. Photographed in July 1996. Due to close in the summer of 1997. *Author*

Type	Date	Signalbox
GN4b	1921	Spalding No1 *(Picture 38)*
GNoSR		
GNoS1	1880	Dyce Junction
GNoS2	1886	Insch
GNoS2	1890	Huntly
GNoS3	1902	Inverurie
GNoS3	1905	Keith Junction
GWR		
GW2	1870s	St Mary's Crossing *(Picture 39)*
GW2	1877	Llanelli West
GW2	1879	Par
GW3	1880s	Ferryside
GW3	1884	Tondu
GW3	1887	Lime Kiln Sidings
GW4b	1883	Ascott-under-Wychwood
GW4b	1883	Moreton-in-Marsh *(Picture 40)*
GW4c	1888	Blakedown
GW5	1892	Aberbeeg Junction
GW5	1892	Neath & B Junction
GW5	1892	Pantyffynnon South
GW5	1893	Lostwithiel
GW5	1894	Tram Inn
GW5	1895	Roskear Junction
GW5	1899	St Erth
GW7	1905	Tunnel Junction
GW7	1907	Pembrey
GW7	1913	Sutton Bridge Junction
GW7a	1899	Truro
GW7a	1900	Newland East
GW7b	1900	Banbury North
GW7b	1901	Stourbridge Junction
GW7c	1906	Clarbeston Road
GW7c	1912	Colthorp Siding
GW7d	1907	Bearley West Junction
GW7d	1907	Droitwich Spa
GW7d	1907	Henley-in-Arden
GW7d	1907	Shirley
GW7d	1908	Banbury South
GW7d	1908	Norton Junction
GW7d	1908	St Blazey Junction
GW7d	1909	Awre
GW7d	1909	Goonbarrow Junction
GW7d	1914	Abbey Foregate
GW7d	1916	Puxton & Worle
GW7d	1918	Greaves Siding
GW7d	1919	Malvern Wells
GW7d	1920	Llandarcy
GW27c	1904	Greenford East Station

Type	Date	Signalbox
GW27c	1905	Pencoed Crossing
GW27c	1905	Croes Newydd North Fork
GW27c	1906	Ashton Junction
GW27c	1910	St Andrews Junction
GW27c	1913	Felin Fran
GW27c	1915	Liskeard
GW27c	1916	Kingswinford Junction South
GW27c	1918	Lydney Crossing
HR		
Highland	1909	Dalwhinnie
Highland	1911	Pitlochry
Highland	1919	Dunkeld
L&SWR		
LSW n/s	1879	Ash Vale Junction
LSW n/s	1898	Waterloo (W&C)
LSW1	1875	Crediton
LSW2	1878	Bollo Lane Junction
LSW3a	1880s	Petersfield *(Picture 41)*
LSW3a	1888	Bournemouth Carriage Sidings
LSW3a	1886	Branksome
LSW3b	1890	Wool
LSW3b	1893	Hamworthy
LSW4	1897	Farncombe
LSW4	1895	Haslemere *(Picture 42)*
LSW4	1897	Poole
LSW4	1901	Farnham
LSW4	1909	Yeovil Junction
LSW4	c1900	Aldershot
L&YR		
L&Y	1890	Cheetham Hill Junction
L&Y	1891	Hebden Bridge *(Picture 43)*
L&Y	1894	Brewery Sidings
L&Y	1896	Blackpool North No2
L&Y	1896	Poulton No3
L&Y	1901	Barnsley Station *(Picture 44)*
L&Y	1901	Crigglestone Junction
L&Y	1902	Huncoat Station
L&Y	1903	Kirkham North Junction
L&Y	1906	Bamber Bridge Station
L&Y	1907	Smithy Bridge
L&Y	1911	Ashton Moss North Junction
L&Y hipped	1905	Dirltdalo
LB&SCR		
LBSC2a	1886	Littlehampton
LBSC2b	1888	Hampden Park
LBSC2b	1891	Plumpton

Above (45):
The only surviving signalbox at Hednesford, photographed in May 1996. *Author*

Left (46):
A variation of the LNWR's standard Type 4 design photographed in June 1996. Mostyn signalbox has a slight overhang. *Author*

Type	Date	Signalbox
LBSC2c	1895	Seaford
LBSC3b	1902	Christ's Hospital
LBSC3b	1911	Barnham
LC&DR		
LCD	1878	Shepherdswell
LNWR		
LNW3	1875	Betley Road
LNW3	1875	Monks Siding
LNW3	1875	Narborough
LNW4	1876	Coundon Road Station
LNW4	1877	Hazel Grove
LNW4	1877	Hednesford No1 *(Picture 45)*
LNW4	1878	Batley

Type	Date	Signalbox
LNW4	1878	Willesden Brent Sidings
LNW4	1879	Parton
LNW4	1880	Llanrwst & Trefriw
LNW4	1881	Prees
LNW4	1882	Gaerwen
LNW4	1882	Wrenbury
LNW4	1882	Harlescott Crossing
LNW4	1883	Fenny Stratford
LNW4	1883	Olive Mount Junction
LNW4	1883	Wem
LNW4	1884	Edgeley Junction No1
LNW4	1884	Edgeley Junction No2
LNW4	1884	Stockport No1
LNW4	1885	Diggle Junction
LNW4	1886	Workington Main No3
LNW4	1887	Furness Vale
LNW4	1888	Denton Junction
LNW4	1888	Greenfield Junction
LNW4	1889	Workington Main No2
LNW4	1890	Stockport No2
LNW4	1891	Llandudno
LNW4	1891	St Helens Station
LNW4	1894	Buxton
LNW4	1894	Hinkley
LNW4	1896	Carterhouse Junction
LNW4	1896	Hawkesbury Lane
LNW4	1897	Prestatyn
LNW4	1897	Basford Hall Junction
LNW4	1897	Halton Junction
LNW4	1897	Lichfield Trent Valley Junction
LNW4	1897	Whitchurch
LNW4	1897	Winsford Junction
LNW4	1899	Alrewas
LNW4	1899	Bransty
LNW4	1899	Gresty Lane No1
LNW4	1899	Hademore Crossing
LNW4	1899	Huyton
LNW4	1900	Canning Street North
LNW4	1900	Helsby Junction
LNW4	1900	Rhyl (No1)
LNW4	1900	Sandycroft
LNW4	1901	Cheadle Hulme
LNW4	1901	Croft Sidings
LNW4	1901	Salop Goods Junction
LNW4	1902	Abergele
LNW4	1902	Holywell Junction
LNW4	1902	Mold Junction No1
LNW4	1902	Mostyn (Picture 46)
LNW4	1903	Shrewsbury Crewe Junction

Above (47):
The gently decaying former signalbox at Llanfair PG, photographed in June 1996. *Author*

Right (48):
Ty Croes former signalbox and station building on the Isle of Anglesey, photographed in June 1996. *Author*

Below right (49):
Amongst other things, the M&GNR used concrete for signalposts and at Cromer built this signalbox partly from concrete blocks. Photographed in June 1996. *Author*

Type	Date	Signalbox
LNW4	1903	Shrewsbury Severn Bridge Junction
LNW4	1903	Talacre
LNW4	1904	Woburn Sands
LNW4	1906	Disley
LNW4	1913	Crosfields Crossing
LNW5	1904	Valley
LNW5	1907	Northampton Bridge Street Level Crossing
LNW5	1907	Speke Junction
LNW5	1908	Brereton Sidings
LNW5	1908	Garston Junction
LNW5	1910	Tamworth Low Level
LNW5	1911	Lichfield Trent Valley No1
LNW5	1912	Frodsham Junction
LNW5	1914	Deganwy
LNW5	1914	Three Spires Junction
LNW5	1915	Beeston Castle & Tarporley
LNW5	1918	Arpley Junction
LNW5	nk	Stechford Shunting Frame

LNWR/Chester & Holyhead Rly

Type	Date	Signalbox
LNW/C&H	1871	Llanfair PG (Picture 47)
LNW/C&H	1872	Ty Croes (Picture 48)

LNW&GWJt

Type	Date	Signalbox
LNW&GWJt 1	1872	Church Stretton
LNW&GWJt 1	1872	Dorrington
LNW&GWJt 1	1872	Marsh Brook
LNW&GWJt 1	1873	Bromfield
LNW&GWJt 1	1875	Leominster
LNW&GWJt 1	1875	Woofferton Junction
LNW&GWJt 2	1884	Hereford

M&CR

Type	Date	Signalbox
M&C	1891	Aspatria

M&GNR

Type	Date	Signalbox
M&GN n/s	1920	Cromer (Picture 49)

MR

Type	Date	Signalbox
Mid2a	1890	Langham Junction
Mid2a	1890	Shirebrook Station
Mid2a	1890	Wennington Junction
Mid2a	1891	Alstone Crossing
Mid2a	1891	Methley Junction
Mid2a	1892	Saxby Junction
Mid2a	1892	Sleights Sidings East
Mid2b	1893	Edale
Mid2b	1893	Totley Tunnel East
Mid2b	1893	Whitwell

Above (50):
Low House Crossing signalbox just outside Armathwaite on the Settle & Carlisle line, photographed in August 1990. *Author*

Right (51):
Swinderby signalbox on the MR's Nottingham to Lincoln line, photographed in March 1991. *Author*

Below right (52):
The only surviving example of the MS&LR's standard signalbox of the 1870s, photographed in September 1987 and due to close in the summer of 1997. *Author*

Type	Date	Signalbox
Mid2b	1895	Acton Canal Wharf
Mid2b	1896	Ecclesfield West
Mid2b	1896	Lowdham
Mid2b	1896	Moira West Junction
Mid2b	1897	Pinxton
Mid2b	1899	Bardon Hill
Mid2b	1899	Neasden Junction
Mid2b	1899	Oakham Level Crossing
Mid2b	1899	Romiley Junction
Mid2b	1899	Shirebrook Junction
Mid2b	1900	Ketton
Mid2b	1900	Low House Crossing *(Picture 50)*
Mid3a	1901	Collingham
Mid3a	1901	Swinderby *(Picture 51)*
Mid3a	1902	Carnforth East Junction
Mid3a	1902	Dudding Hill Junction
Mid3a	1902	Fiskerton
Mid3a	1908	Oddingley
Mid3b	1899	Washwood Heath Sidings No1
Mid3b	1901	Royston Junction
Mid3b	1903	New Mills South Junction
Mid4a	1908	Culgaith
Mid4a	1909	Uffington & Barnack
Mid4a	1912	Ashwell
Mid4a	1912	Newark
Mid4a	1916	Howe & Co's Siding
Mid4a	1916	Lincoln Street
Mid4a	1916	Longbridge East
Mid4c	1908	Moorthorpe
Mid4c	1910	Garsdale
Mid4c	1910	Mantle Lane
Mid4c	1911	Hellifield South Junction
Mid4c	1913	Manton Junction
Mid4c	1913	Settle Junction
Mid4c	1914	Sneinton Junction
MS&LR		
MS&L1	1874	Worksop West *(Picture 52)*
MS&L2	1880	Worksop East
MS&L2	1884	Roxton Sidings
MS&L2	1884	Stallingborough
MS&L2	1885	Gainsborough Central
MS&L2	1888	Penistone *(Picture 53)*
MS&L3	1889	Retford Thrumpton
MS&L3	1890	Holton-le-Moor
MS&L3	1890	Langworth
MS&L3	1890	Wickenby
MS&L3 s/h	1909	Great Coates Sidings No1

Type	Date	Signalbox
NBR		
NB n/s	1899	Swing Bridge East
NB n/s	1906	Usan
NB1	1881	Inverkeilor
NB1	1881	Montrose North
NB1	1881	Montrose South
NB1/4	1886	Sighthill Junction
NB2a	1887	Tay Bridge South
NB4	1882	Carmuirs East Junction
NB4	u1882	Grangemouth Junction
NB4	1901	Cadder
NB6b	1894	Fort William (Mallaig Junction)
NB7	1908	Barry West
NB7	1911	Arbroath North
NB7	1917	Rosyth Dockyard
NB7	nk	Cupar
NB8	1920	Leuchars
NER		
NE C1	1872	Heighington
NE C1	1874	Whitehouse
NE C1	1878	Crag Hall
NE C1	1877	Middlesbrough
NE C2a	1887	Shildon
NE C2a	1896	Urlay Nook
NE C2a	1897	Norton-on-Tees
NE C2a	1904	Billingham
NE C2a	1905	Cemetery North
NE C2b	1903	Nunthorpe
NE n/s	1869	Goole Bridge
NE n/s	1870	Norton East
NE n/s	1870	Norton South
NE n/s	1873	Knaresborough
NE n/s	1891	Selby Swing Bridge
NE n/s	1904	Clarence Road
NE n/s	1905	Bowesfield
NE n/s	c1872	North Seaton
NE N1	1870s	East Boldon
NE N1	1872	Prudhoe
NE N1	1874	Bardon Mill
NE N1	1877	Haydon Bridge
NE N1	1874	Low Row
NE N1	1896	Ashington
NE N1	1889	Greatham
NE N1	1893	Boldon Colliery
NE N1	nk	Bedlington South
NE N1	nk	Newsham South
NE N1	c1876	Monkwearmouth
NE N2	1893	Milton
NE N2	1895	Marcheys House

Type	Date	Signalbox
NE N2	1895	Winning
NE N2	nk	Blaydon
NE N3	1905	Dawdon
NE N3	1905	Hall Dene
NE N3	1905	Ryhope Grange Junction
NE N3	1905	Seaham
NE N3	1907	Alnmouth
NE N4	1911	Stranton
NE N4	1912	Bedlington North
NE N4	c1918	Brampton Fell
NE N5 overhead	c1918	Hexham
NE N5 overhead	1897	Wylam
NE S1	1870s	Poppleton
NE S1	1870	Selby
NE S1	1882	Castleford Station
NE S1	1882	Castleford Gates
NE S1a	1873	Hemingbrough
NE S1a	1873	Howden
NE S1a	1873	Kirkham Abbey
NE S1a	1873	Malton
NE S1a	1873	Moss
NE S1a	1873	Picton
NE S1a	1873	Weaverthorpe
NE S1a	1873	Thorpe Gates
NE S1a	c1873	Rigton
NE S1a	1875	Bedale
NE S1a	1875	Driffield
NE S1a	1875	Bridlington South
NE S1a	1875	Hunmanby

Opposite (53):
The exposed wooden supports of this elevated signalbox at Penistone (originally named Huddersfield Junction) were replaced in the 1970s with brick pillars. Photographed in July 1996. *Author*

Above (54):
The former NER signalbox at Oxmardyke, photographed in November 1989. *Author*

Centre left (55):
Gilberdyke Junction, photographed in November 1989. *Author*

Bottom left (56):
Falsgrave signalbox at Scarborough, photographed in September 1988. It still contains a 120-lever McKenzie & Holland frame. *Author*

Type	Date	Signalbox
NE S1a	1898	Barlby
NE S1a	1901	Oxmardyke (Picture 54)
NE S1a	1912	Henwick Hall
NE S1a	nk	Starbeck South
NE S1a	c1873	Peckfield
NE S1b	1873	Gristhorpe
NE S1b	1873	Howsham
NE S1b	1873	Long Lane
NE S1b	1883	Horsforth
NE S1b	1890	Whitwood
NE S1b	1891	Crabley Creek
NE S2	1901	Strensall
NE S2	1903	Gilberdyke Junction (Picture 55)
NE S2	1904	Broomfleet
NE S2	1904	Brough East
NE S2	1904	Welton
NE S2	1905	Saltmarshe
NE S3	1904	Church Fenton
NE S4	1904	Cave
NE S4	1906	Seamer West
NE S4	1908	Cayton
NE S4	1908	Falsgrave (Scarborough) (Picture 56)
NE S4	1908	Gascoigne Wood
NE S4	1909	Goole
NE S4	1910	Seamer East
NE S4	1911	Beverley Station
NE S4	1911	Filey
NE S4	1911	Quay Crossing (Bridlington)
NE S4	1921	Melton Lane
NE S4	c1921	Norton West
NE S5	1910	Marston Moor
NE S5	1914	Belmont
NE S5	nk	Cattal

(The NER types are divided into Northern (N), Central (C) and Southern (S) Divisions.)

NLR		
NL3a	1891	Western Junction
NL3a	1892	Acton Wells Junction
NL3b	1896	Camden Road Junction
NL3b	1900	Kew East Junction

NSR		
NS1	1877	Egginton Junction
NS1	1880	Meaford Crossing
NS1	1885	Sudbury
NS2	1889	Bradwell Sidings
NS2	1889	Foley Crossing
NS2	nk	Leigh
NS2	nk	Mow Cop
NS2	1880s	Scropton

Type	Date	Signalbox
SER		
SE	1880s	Chartham
SE	1892	East Farleigh
SE	nk	Cuxton
SE	1870s	Snodland
SE	c1912	Bopeep Junction
SE	c1904	Stone Crossing
SE&CR		
SEC	c1911	Canterbury East *(Picture 57)*
SEC	1913	Gillingham
TVR		
Taff Vale	1899	Radyr Quarry Junction
Taff Vale	1900	Llandaff Loop Junction
Taff Vale	1902	Pontypridd Junction
Taff Vale	1910s	Walnut Tree Junction

Above (57):
Canterbury East, photographed in August 1975.
J. Scrace

4. INTERWAR SIGNALBOXES 1923-1940

With the Grouping of the railway companies in 1923, some form of standardisation might have been expected. In fact, money was not available for much new building and what new standards did appear — and each company had more than one — only added to the variety of designs. The number of independent signalling contractors was much reduced, and following the Grouping, although they continued to supply equipment, it was always installed in signal-boxes designed by the railway companies.

At first these designs were very conservative and derived from established pre-Grouping examples, but during the 1930s

companies became more adventurous. Some, naturally, were more adventurous than others. The GWR's daring only extended to providing its new powerboxes at Paddington (1933) and Bristol Temple Meads (1935) with flat roofs. The LNER was undecided, choosing

Right (58):
Sessay Wood signalbox was just completed when this photograph was taken in April 1933 to record resignalling work on the LNER's York to Newcastle stretch of line. *Modern Transport*

Below (59):
The SR's signalbox at Arundel, opened in 1938 and still looking modern when photographed 30 years later. *J. Scrace*

Below right (60):
The LMSR standard signalbox of the 1930s politically incorporated both LNWR and MR features. Maryport exhibits an LNWR brick base and pitched roof, and MR-style timber work. Photographed in May 1996. *Author*

in 1933 both a modern flat roof design for Thirsk powerbox and a more homely pitched roof 'Garden City'-style for Sessay Wood (renamed Pilmoor South in 1943) and other new mechanical boxes north of York. *(Picture 58)*

Only the SR truly captured the spirit of the period with what have since been dubbed its 'Glasshouse' or 'Odeon Style' signalboxes. With flat concrete roofs, bold semicircular ends, and their names prominently displayed on the fronts from moulded concrete, the new SR signalboxes were, like the cinemas that inspired them, genuinely modern. *(Picture 59)* These bold structures were used by the SR to house either traditional lever frames, or where new colour light signalling was installed, miniature levers as well.

The following is a list of surviving signalboxes built to interwar designs still in operation, with the type numbers allocated to them by the Signalling Record Society. (Preserved structures are not included.)

Type	Date	Signalbox
GW11	1935	Worcester Shrub Hill
GW11	1937	Yeovil Pen Mill
GW12	1939	Cosford
GW12a	1941	Bishton Crossing
GW12a	1943	Moreton-on-Lugg
GW12b	1938	Penzance
GW27c	1933	Stratford-on-Avon
GW27c s/h	1932	Abercynon
GW28	1929	Codsall
GW28	1930	Maesmawr
GW28b	1932	Bentley Heath Crossing
GW28b	1934	Abergavenny
(GW27 & 28 were developments of a pre-Grouping design)		
LMS n/s	1929	Deal Street
LMS11	1930	Forders Sidings
LMS11b	1930	Madeley
LMS11b	1932	Southend East
LMS11b	1933	Eccles
LMS11b	1933	Hickleton Main Colliery
LMS11b	1933	Maryport *(Picture 60)*
LMS11b s/h	1952	Cark
LMS11c	1933	Rainford Junction

Left (61):
The all-timber LMSR signalboxes were closer in style to their MR predecessors. Melton Mowbray signalbox, photographed in June 1996. *Author*

Below right (62):
The attractive LNER signalbox at Brandon, Norfolk, photographed in June 1996. *Author*

Below left (63):
Signalboxes that straddled the track were once not unusual. This is one of the few surviving examples at Canterbury West, photographed in September 1967. *J. Scrace*

Bottom (64):
Reigate signalbox opened in 1929 before the SR adopted a more progressive look for new buildings. Photographed in June 1969. *J. Scrace*

Type	Date	Signalbox
LMS11c	1934	Grindleford
LMS11c	1935	Crewe Steel Works
LMS11c	1937	Bare Lane
LMS11c	1939	Longport Junction
LMS11c	1941	Blea Moor
LMS11c	1941	Frisby Station
LMS11c	1941	Stanlow & Thornton
LMS11c	1942	Caverswall
LMS11c	1942	Melton Station *(Picture 61)*
LMS11c	1946	Elmton & Cresswell
LMS11c	1950	Staythorpe Crossing
LMS11c	1951	Appleby North
LMS11c	1953	Willesden Carriage Shed Middle
LMS11c	1953	Willesden Carriage Shed North
LMS11c	1953	Willesden Carriage Shed South
LMS11c s/h	1948	Nantwich
LMS11e	1937	Holyhead Station
LMS12	1920s	Hurlford
LMS12	1927	Dunragit
LMS12	1929	Longforgan
LMS12	1929	Lugton
LMS12	1933	Blackford
LNER11b	1931	Bishop's Stortford South
LNER n/s	1924	East Gate Junction
LNER n/s	1927	Ranelagh Road Crossing
LNER11a	1926	Keadby Canal Junction
LNER11a	1926	Woodhouse East Junction
LNER11a	1927	March South Junction
LNER11a	1937	Scopwick
LNER11a	c1927	Highams Park
LNER11b	1939	Saxilby
LNER11c	1931	Brandon *(Picture 62)*
LNER11c	1931	Gidea Park
LNER11c	1931	Romford
LNER12	1932	Longbeck
LNER13	1936	Barton Hill
LNER13	1937	Redcar
LNER13PB	1938	Hull Paragon
SR n/s	1928	Bournemouth
SR overhead	1928	Canterbury West *(Picture 63)*
SR (signalbox and booking office)	1938	Littlehaven
SR11a	1921	Aylesford
SR11a	1923	Betteshanger Colliery
SR11a	1926	Ramsgate
SR11a	1928	Archcliffe Junction
SR11b	1929	Reigate *(Picture 64)*
SR11b	1938	Sandwich
SR12	1929	Minster
SR12	1930	Dover Priory

Type	Date	Signalbox
SR12	1930	Hastings
SR12	1933	Wokingham
SR12	1934	Hawkesbury Station Junction
SR13	1937	Woking
SR13	1938	Arundel
SR13	1938	Bognor Regis
SR13	1938	Dorking
SR13	1938	Horsham
SR13	1938	Templecombe
SR13	1939	Deal
SR13	1939	New Hythe
SR13	1940	Richmond

5. POSTWAR SIGNALBOXES 1945-1985

During World War 2 a number of signalboxes at what were believed to be vulnerable locations had brick anti-blast walls constructed around their locking rooms. New boxes were also designed to withstand enemy attack, the standard ARP signalbox of the LMSR, for example, incorporating a flat concrete roof over a foot thick. *(Pictures 65 & 66)*

After the war, the new British Railways failed to produce a standard signalbox design. In some ways this is not surprising as the future indicated that the day of the individual mechanical signalbox controlling semaphores and the block system were

Right (65):
Shrewsbury Crewe Bank built to LMSR ARP design in 1943, and photographed in June 1996. *Author*

Below right (66):
Wigan Wallgate, opened by the LMSR in 1941. Photographed in May 1996. *Author*

Far right (67):
Birmingham New Street powerbox, recently added to the list of protected buildings considered of architectural merit. *London Midland Region (BR)*

numbered, and the trend was going to be towards the control of increasingly larger areas with colour light signals and electrically-operated points activated from 'power signalboxes' fitted with panels of switches or buttons. With the publication of the 1955 Modernisation Report, the aim of building and equipping a number of strategically located powerboxes all over the network so that hundreds of mechanical signalboxes could be abolished became a recognised goal. A number of schemes were successfully completed, and the list on pages 50-58 which includes many of those powerboxes, is a testament to what was achieved. Not all went according to plan, of course. The West Coast main line continues, embarrassingly, to illustrate the compromises that had to be made in order to start running electric trains over this route in the 1960s. Powerboxes were successfully commissioned at a number of places, the most impressive opening at Birmingham New Street in 1966. (Pictures 67 & 68) Wilmslow powerbox opened in 1959, but only a few miles away at Stockport, the LNWR's two huge structures of 1884 and 1890 still remain

containing a total of 186 levers despite the reduction of both frames. (Pictures 69 & 70) Nuneaton powerbox opened in 1963, but further along the Trent Valley line, the LNWR's Tamworth Low Level mechanical signalbox survives in constant use as does Lichfield Trent Valley No 1. (Picture 71)

Whether powerboxes or ordinary mechanical signalboxes, what new structures were built in this period were more often than not design one-offs, although certain types confined to the Regions were used more than once. The Signalling Record Society has tried to bring some order to the varieties, but it must be noted that there were subtle differences between boxes of supposedly the same design.

The most prolific 'standard' (of which many examples still survive) was what the SRS has termed the LM Region's Type 15. It was the type which Triang used for its model signalbox in the 1960s. The design first appeared in 1954 and, with its overhanging flat roof, it had something in common with the LMSR wartime design. Like MR boxes, it was based on standard modules so that structures of various sizes could be

Above (68):
The NX (Entrance/Exit) panel inside Birmingham New Street powerbox soon after commissioning. *London Midland Region (BR)*

Below (69):
The LNWR's Stockport No 1 signalbox photographed in July 1996. *Author*

Opposite (70):
Stockport No 2 on the same day. *Author*

Opposite below (71):
No 87031 *Hal o' the Wynd* speeds passed Lichfield Trent Valley No 1 signalbox on 4 August 1996. *Author*

constructed. *(Picture 72)* Despite its sensible and pleasing design, it was only ever used to house mechanical lever frames. When panels were to be used to operate signals and points, they were installed in completely different structures.

In this period, whether mechanical or not, signalboxes reflected, to varying degrees, the prevailing architectural fashion. Stafford No 5 (1952) and Wellington No 2 (1953) are both humane, well-proportioned examples from the 'Harlow New Town' period. *(Pictures 73 & 74)* Netherfield Junction (1960) and particularly Hubberts Bridge (1961) are uncompromising examples of the then popular 'brutalist' style. *(Pictures 75 & 76)* Guildford powerbox of 1966 is undoubtedly a child of its time.*(Picture 77)* A decade later, Claypole (1977) and other gateboxes like it on the East Coast main line, marked the end of this period of architecture just as the post-modern movement was beginning to become influential. *(Picture 78)*

Above (72):
Colwich Junction on the West Coast main line, photographed in May 1996. The extension to the relay room was not a standard feature of this design. *Author*

Right (73):
Stafford No 5 photographed in June 1996. *Author*

Below right (74):
Wellington No 2, photographed in June 1996 and now the only signalbox at this station after No 3 and 4 closed on 30 September 1973. *Author*

Bottom right (75):
Netherfield Junction just outside Nottingham, photographed in June 1996. *Author*

Left (76):
Hubberts Bridge signalbox on the ex-GNR line between Sleaford and Boston. Photographed in June 1996. *Author*

Below (77):
Guildford powerbox, photographed when new in 1966. *BR(SR)*

Bottom (78):
The gatebox on the site of the former GNR station at Claypole, photographed in August 1996. *Author*

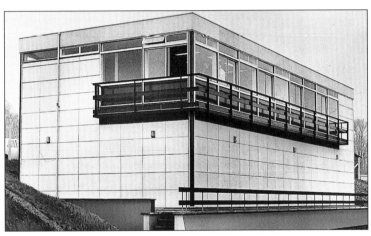

The following is a list of surviving signalboxes on the national network built between 1945 and 1985, with the type numbers allocated to them by the Signalling Record Society. (Preserved boxes are not included.)

Type	Date	Signalbox
BR(ER) n/s	1959	Dodworth
BR(ER) n/s	1959	Harringay Park Junction
BR(ER) n/s	1960	Netherfield Junction
BR(ER) n/s	1961	Hubberts Bridge
BR(ER) n/s	1965	Brightside
BR(ER) n/s	1972	Scunthorpe Hump
BR(ER) n/s	1975	Cutsyke Junction
BR(ER)16a	1957	Sleaford South
BR(ER)16a	1958	Pyewipe Road
BR(ER)16a	1959	Oxmarsh Crossing *(Picture 79)*
BR(ER)18	1960	Ware
BR(ER)18PB	1960	Broxbourne
BR(ER)18PB	1960	Hackney Downs
BR(ER)18PB	1960	Harlow Mill
BR(ER)18PB	1961	Witham
BR(ER)18PB	1965	Tinsley Yard
BR(ER)18PB	1965	West Burton
BR(ER)19	1961	Pasture Street
BR(ER)19	1963	Seymour Junction
BR(ER)19	1964	Gainsborough Trent Junction
BR(ER)20	1975	Holme
BR(ER)20	1975	Tallington
BR(ER)20	1976	Everton
BR(ER)20	1976	Offord
BR(ER)20	1977	Barnby

Type	Date	Signalbox
BR(ER)20	1977	Carlton
BR(ER)20	1977	Claypole
BR(ER)20	1978	Morpeth
BR(ER)20	1980	Norton
BR(ER)PB	1961	Barking
BR(ER)PB	1963	Healey Mills
BR(ER)PB	1971	King's Cross
BR(ER)PB	1972	Peterborough
BR(ER)PB	1973	Scunthorpe
BR(ER)PB	1973	Sheffield
BR(ER)PB	1979	Doncaster
BR(ER)PB	1982	Cambridge
BR(ER)PB	1983	Colchester
BR(LMR) n/s	1959	Chelford Frame
BR(LMR) n/s	1961	Weaver Junction
BR(LMR) n/s	1985	Gospel Oak
BR(LMR)14	1949	Stapleford & Sandiacre (Picture 80)
BR(LMR)14	1951	Bestwood Park Junction
BR(LMR)14	1952	Penmaenmawr
BR(LMR)14	1952	Stafford No5
BR(LMR)14	1954	Vitriol Works
BR(LMR)14	1955	Heaton Norris Junction
BR(LMR)15	1955	Lock Lane Crossing
BR(LMR)15	1956	Atherton Goods Yard
BR(LMR)15	1956	Ditton Junction No1
BR(LMR)15	1956	Grange-over-Sands
BR(LMR)15	1957	Aston SCC
BR(LMR)15	1957	Chapel-en-le-Frith
BR(LMR)15	1957	Deansgate Junction
BR(LMR)15	1957	Rock Ferry
BR(LMR)15	1957	Vauxhall Shunting Frame
BR(LMR)15	1957	Wigton
BR(LMR)15	1958	Corkickle No1
BR(LMR)15	1958	Corkickle No2
BR(LMR)15	1958	Hest Bank
BR(LMR)15	1959	Blackpool North No1
BR(LMR)15	1959	Bloxwich (Picture 81)
BR(LMR)15	1960	Allerton Junction
BR(LMR)15	1960	Ditton Junction No2
BR(LMR)15	1960	Stafford No4
BR(LMR)15	1961	Colwich
BR(LMR)15	1961	Glazebrook East Junction
BR(LMR)15	1962	Crewe Sort Sidings North
BR(LMR)15	1963	Bescot Up Hump
BR(LMR)15	1963	Castleton East Junction
BR(LMR)15	1963	Flag Lane
BR(LMR)15	1964	Acton Lane
BR(LMR)15	1964	Tring Carriage Sidings Frame
BR(LMR)15	1965	Ashton OA&GB Junction
BR(LMR)15	1965	Kidsgrove Central

Above (80):
Built as part of the modernisation of Toton yard at the end of World War 2, Stapleford & Sandiacre opened as a signalbox in 1949, and was downgraded to a shunting frame when Trent powerbox was commissioned a few miles away in 1969. *Author*

Right (81):
Bloxwich signalbox, photographed in May 1996. *Author*

Below right (82):
Unless you know what you are looking at, Huddersfield powerbox just looks like a modern addition to the station. Photographed in July 1996. *Author*

Type	Date	Signalbox
BR(LMR)15	1965	Macclesfield
BR(LMR)15	1966	Curzon Street
BR(LMR)15	1966	Grange Junction
BR(LMR)15	1967	Fiddlers Ferry Power Station
BR(LMR)15	1968	Holyhead
BR(LMR)15	1969	Drakelow CEGB Sidings
BR(LMR)15	1969	Garston FL Frame
BR(LMR)15	1969	Kingsbury Shunting Frame
BR(LMR)15	1969	Madeley Junction
BR(LMR)15	1969	Mickle Trafford
BR(LMR)15	1969	Oxley
BR(LMR)15	1969	Stanton Gate
BR(LMR)15	1972	Crow Nest Junction
BR(LMR)15	1972	Ellesmere Port No4
BR(LMR)15	1972	Midge Hall
BR(LMR)15	1972	Norton
BR(LMR)15	1972	Penyffordd
BR(LMR)15	1974	Kirkby Stephen West
BR(LMR)15	1974	Norbury Crossing
BR(LMR)15	1975	Greenbank
BR(LMR)15	1977	Bedford St Johns No1
BR(LMR)15	1980	Chinley
BR(LMR)15	1981	Uttoxeter
BR(LMR)15	1985	Llandudno Junction
BR(LMR)15	nk	Ribble Yard
BR(LMR)15 s/h	1967	Oldham Mumps
BR(LMR)15 s/h	1972	Astley
BR(LMR)15 s/h	1973	Warrington Central
BR(LMR)PB	1959	Sandbach
BR(LMR)PB	1959	Wilmslow
BR(LMR)PB	1961	Edge Hill
BR(LMR)PB	1961	Norton Bridge
BR(LMR)PB	1962	Coventry
BR(LMR)PB	1962	Manchester Victoria East Junction
BR(LMR)PB	1963	Kingmoor
BR(LMR)PB	1963	Nuneaton
BR(LMR)PB	1964	Rugby
BR(LMR)PB	1964	Watford
BR(LMR)PB	1965	Bescot Down Tower
BR(LMR)PB	1965	Bletchley
BR(LMR)PB	1965	Euston
BR(LMR)PB	1965	Walsall
BR(LMR)PB	1965	Willesden
BR(LMR)PB	1965	Wolverhampton
BR(LMR)PB	1966	Birmingham New Street
BR(LMR)PB	1966	Stoke
BR(LMR)PB	1969	Derby
BR(LMR)PB	1969	Saltley
BR(LMR)PB	1969	Trent
BR(LMR)PB	1972	Preston

Type	Date	Signalbox
BR(LMR)PB	1972	Warrington
BR(LMR)PB	1973	Carlisle
BR(LMR)PB	1979	Cricklewood Depot
BR(LMR)PB	1979	West Hampstead
BR(LMR)PB	1984	Chester
BR(LMR)PB	1985	Crewe Signalling Centre
BR(LMR)PB	1985	Leamington Spa
BR(NER)13	1950	Ferryhill
BR(NER)16b	1954	Wardley
BR(NER)16b	1956	Ferrybridge
BR(NER)16b	1956	Freemans
BR(NER)16b	1956	Low Gates
BR(NER)17	1955	Corby Gates
BR(NER)17	1957	Balne
BR(NER)17	1957	Milford
BR(NER)17	1958	Cliff House
BR(NER)17	1958	Elland
BR(NER)17	1959	Sudforth Lane
BR(NER)17	1967	Knottingley
BR(NER)PB	1958	Huddersfield (Picture 82)
BR(NER)PB	1958	Shaftholme Junction
BR(NER)PB	1961	Tweedmouth
BR(NER)PB	1962	Hessle Road
BR(NER)PB	1965	Sunderland
BR(ScR) n/s	1961	Stanley Junction
BR(ScR) n/s	1963	Annat
BR(ScR) n/s	1969	Longannet
BR(ScR)16c	1955	Dumfries South
BR(ScR)16c	1956	Cowlairs
BR(ScR)16c	1957	Dumfries
BR(ScR)PB	1961	Cathcart
BR(ScR)PB	1961	Glasgow Central
BR(ScR)PB	1962	Perth
BR(ScR)PB	1966	Paisley (Picture 83)
BR(ScR)PB	1972	Motherwell
BR(ScR)PB	1976	Edinburgh SC
BR(ScR)PB	1976	Kilmarnock
BR(ScR)PB	1981	Aberdeen
BR(ScR)PB	1985	Dundee SC
BR(ScR)PB	1985	Paisley
BR(SR) n/s	1953	Snowdown Colliery
BR(SR) n/s	1970	Northfleet
BR(SR)16	1954	Shalford
BR(SR)16	1957	Gillingham
BR(SR)16	1957	Honiton
BR(SR)16	1959	Dorchester
BR(SR)16	1963	Lancing
BR(SR)17PB	1959	Rochester (Picture 84)
BR(SR)17PB	1959	Barnes
BR(SR)17PB	1959	Faversham

Type	Date	Signalbox
BR(SR)17PB	1959	Rainham
BR(SR)17PB	1959	Sittingbourne
BR(SR)18	1959	Exmouth Junction
BR(SR)18	1962	Maidstone East
BR(SR)18	1964	Brockenhurst
BR(SR)18	1966	Ash Crossing
BR(SR)18PB	1962	Folkestone Junction
BR(SR)18PB	1962	Hither Green
BR(SR)18PB	1962	Tonbridge *(Picture 85)*
BR(SR)19PB	1966	Basingstoke
BR(SR)19PB	1966	Eastleigh
BR(SR)19PB	1966	Guildford
BR(SR)19PB	1968	Portsmouth
BR(SR)19PB	1970	Surbiton
BR(SR)PB	1970	Dartford
BR(SR)PB	1974	Feltham
BR(SR)PB	1975	London Bridge
BR(SR)PB	1980	Victoria Signalling Centre
BR(SR)PB	1981	Eastleigh
BR(SR)PB	1983	Three Bridges
BR(WR) n/s	1981	Porth
BR(WR) n/s	1982	Chard Junction
BR(WR)15	1951	Lightmoor Junction

Right (83):
Paisley powerbox no longer controls trains, but this is what it looked like shortly after it was commissioned in 1966. *BR(ScR)*

Below right (84):
Rochester powerbox was only 12 years old when this photograph was taken in May 1971. *Ian Allan Library*

Type	Date	Signalbox
BR(WR)15	1953	Wellington No2
BR(WR)16	1953	Kidderminster Junction *(Picture 86)*
BR(WR)16a	1956	Carmarthen Junction
BR(WR)17	1960	Fenny Compton
BR(WR)35	1950s	Kidwelly
BR(WR)37	1960	Machynlleth
BR(WR)37	1961	East Usk
BR(WR)37	1977	Onibury
BR(WR)37 s/h	1961	Radyr Junction
BR(WR)37a	1957	Evesham
BR(WR)37b s/h	1970	Bargoed
BR(WR)37b s/h	1972	Whitland
BR(WR)PB	1960	Plymouth
BR(WR)PB	1962	Newport
BR(WR)PB	1962	Old Oak Common
BR(WR)PB	1963	Port Talbot
BR(WR)PB	1963	Slough
BR(WR)PB	1965	Reading
BR(WR)PB	1966	Cardiff
BR(WR)PB	1968	Gloucester
BR(WR)PB	1968	Swindon *(Picture 87)*
BR(WR)PB	1970	Bristol
BR(WR)PB	1973	Oxford
BR(WR)PB	1984	Westbury
BR(WR)PB	1985	Exeter

Right (85):
Another child of the 1960s, Tonbridge powerbox under construction in early 1961. *BR(SR)*

Below right (86):
After years of conservative design, the successors to the GWR finally broke with tradition in the 1950s with structures like this one at Kidderminster Junction. Photographed in July 1996. *Author*

Opposite top (87):
Swindon powerbox could not have been further from ex-GWR aesthetics when it was built in 1968. For such a comparatively recent building it has certainly dated very rapidly. *BR(WR)*

axlebox detectors reduced the need for signalmen to see passing trains, but powerboxes were still fitted with windows. Now with the increased use of permanently coupled trains and multiple-unit working, it has obviously been decided that signalman do not need to see outside at all, nor actually work near the railway. When Westbury powerbox opened in 1984 there were features of the post-modern design that indicated that it was obviously a signalbox: it still had windows and was near to passing trains. *(Picture 88)* A year later the new Crewe Signalling Centre could have been mistaken for an industrial unit — because it was an industrial unit! *(Picture 89)* York Integrated Electronic Control Centre (IECC) (1989) is a similar structure well away from the lineside and is a far cry from what NER management would have considered proper. The recently opened signalling centre at Sandhills, Liverpool, is another example of this continuing trend. *(Picture 90)* The increased use of solid state interlocking and VDUs will reduce still further the need for special buildings.

But perhaps the ultimate anonymous building, the name of which actually indicates its temporary nature, is the Portakabin. Since 1981, nine of these prefabricated structures have been used to house signalling panels, and more might be used in the future:

6. MODERN SIGNALBOXES AND SIGNALLING CENTRES 1985-

There are three reasons for choosing 1985 as the beginning of this latest phase in the evolution of the signalbox. The first two concern design, and the third involves attitudes to reuse.

In 1985 the last new mechanical signalbox was opened on British Rail, a BR(LMR)15, at Llandudno Junction. It is unlikely that any mechanical signalboxes with frames of interlocking levers will be built again, other than on preserved railways.

The year 1985 could also be said to have marked the end of the construction of recognisable signalboxes. Until then signalboxes were still built by the lineside and, no matter how unusual the architecture, it was not too difficult to identify their purpose. Continuous track circuiting, the very basis of modern signalling, lineside telephones and hot

Type	Date	Signalbox
Stourton	BR(WR)	1981
Wakefield	BR(ER)	1982
Heath Junction	BR(WR)	1984
Stonea	BR(ER)	1984
Barlaston (G)	BR(LMR)	1985
Hooton	BR(LMR)	1985
Upper Holloway	BR(ER)	1985
Rufford	BR(LMR)	1988
Skiers Spring	BR(ER)	1990

So that this chapter does not end on a completely dismal note, the final reason for choosing 1985 is because in the 1980s there appeared to be a move away from the demolition of mechanical signalboxes when their frames were removed and the surrounding signalling was upgraded. Until then it had been the usual practice, when changing from mechanical signalling to colour lights, to demolish boxes and install new control panels in completely new structures. During the 1980s, it became more common for old signalboxes to survive without their mechanical frames but with new panels. *(Picture 91)* Studying the list of signalboxes in Chapter 6 will indicate this. Inevitably, however, only time will tell whether this trend will continue, and whether it is really cost-effective to maintain brick and timber buildings when Railtrack can buy off-the-shelf indestructible industrial units.

Despite the recent trend towards the installation of signalling control panels in industrial units and Portakabins, the majority of surviving signalboxes still conform to a recognisable building type.

Most manual signalboxes are at least two storeys high with continuous glazing around at least two sides. This configuration was the result not only of the need to give signalmen a good view of the tracks they supervised, but also due to the construction of the lever frame installed inside. *(Picture 92)*

A. THE OPERATING FLOOR

Judging from the photographs that survive, some of the first levers used at ground level to move points had their fulcrums only a few inches above the platforms they were attached to. When Saxby developed his 'Simultaneous Motion' frame in 1856, the levers operating the semaphores were of this design, but the point levers were pivoted a few feet below the signalman to make them mechanically more efficient. The signalman stood on the 'operating floor', with half the length of the point lever underneath him. This meant that the operating floor had to be elevated above ground level. Saxby's first interlocked frame of 1860 perpetuated the

Below (92):
Ironbridge & Broseley signalbox on the Severn Valley line of the GWR, photographed early in the 20th century. *T. Blood Collection*

difference in the length of signal and point levers, but subsequent designs, and all of those manufactured by rival firms and railway companies except one, had levers of the same dimensions which passed through, and were pivoted beneath, the operating floor. The only significant exception to this arrangement was to be found in frames made by the MR from the 1870s onwards, which contained levers pivoted at operating floor level. Even so, MR signalboxes along with their contemporaries were usually buildings of two distinct levels, the operating floor usually accessed by an external flight of wooden steps.

B. THE LOCKING ROOM
On the first lever frames of the 1860s, the interlocking to prevent conflicting signals being given was usually immediately behind the levers. With the notable exception of MR and Saxby & Farmer's 'Rocker' and 'Rocker & Gridiron' frames, by the 1870s interlocking on the majority of lever frames was beneath the operating floor in the lower room.

Above (93):
The locking trays and horizontal tappet bars beneath the operating floor of Crewe Junction, Shrewsbury. Photographed during an official visit in May 1984. *Author*

Opposite (94):
The relay room of Bow Junction signalbox, photographed in September 1949. *BR/Topical*

Thereafter, this room was invariably referred to as the 'locking room'.

The complexity of the interlocking between levers often dictated the size and shape of locking rooms. In the two decades leading up to World War 1 some of the largest manual lever frames ever constructed were installed in new signalboxes. The interlocking between levers was necessarily complex and took up much space, and so the trays of locks and tappet blades were either

laid out horizontally and the locking rooms made wide to accommodate them, or they were set out vertically in locking rooms of more than one storey high. *(Picture 93)*

The locking room also accommodated the counterbalance weights on the 'tails' of the levers, and through a gap at the base of the wall, usually at the front of the signalbox, exited the wires (sometimes chains) and rods connecting the levers to the external equipment they operated.

C. LOCKING ROOM TO RELAY ROOM

As the mechanical lever frame reached its physical limits of development at the beginning of the 20th century, the advantages of operating signals and points either electrically, pneumatically or by other means were becoming obvious. Levers could then act as simple switches to turn motors, or valves, on and off. They could be miniaturised or replaced by other forms of handle, and where mechanical interlocking was still used, this could be brought out of the locking room and onto the operating floor.

The locking rooms did not empty completely, however. Eventually developments went a stage further and interlocking itself was achieved through electrical relays. The locking room of the traditional signalbox then became the 'relay room' of the new 'power signalbox'. After World War 2, compared to the operating floor with its compact panel of switches or buttons, relay rooms increased dramatically in size to accommodate the hundreds of relays needed to control increasingly large areas of track. *(Picture 94)* As a result, the operating room of a signalbox was often smaller than the relay room supporting it. It was not until the solid-state revolution of the 1980s that miniaturisation reduced the overall size of signalboxes.

D. THE STRUCTURE

The majority of pre-Grouping signalboxes were built between 1870 and 1890. When railway companies committed themselves to interlocking and the block system (both made compulsory by the 1889 Regulation of Railways Act), that inevitably resulted in the

construction of thousands of signalboxes. That most companies developed standard designs in this period was not just because of a desire to establish a corporate identity, but because standardisation of materials and dimensions was a fundamental way of keeping building costs down.

During the 1870s and 80s, all railway companies built signalboxes to no more than a few standard designs. All the common building materials of the day were used: brick, stone, timber, tile, slate and glass, in various combinations ranging from all-brick to all-timber structures. The choice of materials seems to have been a purely company preference, varying from time to time, and not related to weather or local geographical conditions. Timber was used as much in Scotland as brick was in Devon and Cornwall.

There were, however, a number of benefits to building all-timber (or predominantly timber) structures. Once erected, they could be resited if necessary (though this rarely happened). More importantly, parts could be prefabricated and stored in 'kit form' until needed for either new or replacement work. It was obviously of benefit for signalling contractors to operate in this way, the speed with which they could respond to contract work making their tenders more competitive. Standard-sized prefabricated building sections were also slightly more flexible from a practical view-point than a standard design for a complete building. Standard units could be fitted together to create not only standard but non-standard buildings when necessary. Some railway companies, most notably the MR, L&YR, and to some extent the LNWR, also favoured modular timber designs. Of these, the MR, with very few exceptions, remained faithful to prefabricated timber signalboxes for over 50 years. Although it has been quoted before in *The Signal Box* (OPC), it is worth relating again that it was the MR who dramatically demonstrated another benefit of building with prefabricated units by erecting Souldrop signalbox in just 1hr 25min in June 1920.

The only other material from which you

could produce a finished signalbox in so short a time was concrete. During the 1930s, the GWR built a number of boxes from prefabricated and precast concrete sections and then during the 1950s and 1960s, modular construction was used for a number of new powerboxes.

E. INSTRUMENTATION

As outlined in the previous chapter (and in more detail in abc Signalling in the Age of Steam) the lever frame and associated mechanical equipment developed separately from the electrical devices to control the 'block system'. When the two were first brought together in the signalboxes of the 1860s, the separation was perpetuated. Lever frames were almost always located in the front of signalboxes, ie nearest the running lines, but instruments were either installed opposite or at right angles to them, often on the top of cupboards or the signalmen's lockers on the operating floor.

During the next decade, a number of attempts were made to physically link the block instruments with the lever frame, so that the procedures for passing trains

between signalboxes could be made compulsory. This form of control was called 'lock & block', and one of the most successful systems that emerged was patented by William Sykes in 1875 and 1880. His instruments were fixed to shelves suspended over the lever frames, so that rods could connect the equipment. By the 1880s, even if Sykes' 'lock & block' was not installed, it was usual to find instruments mounted on 'block shelves' over the levers. A number of railway companies then felt that this combination of lever frame and instrumentation obstructed a signalman's view of the track, and there was a trend at the end of the 19th century towards the installation of frames and block instruments at the back of boxes.

Below (95):
The operating floor of the GWR's Kennington Junction signalbox, photographed in the 1950s. Opened in 1901, the box closed in December 1973. *Author's Collection*

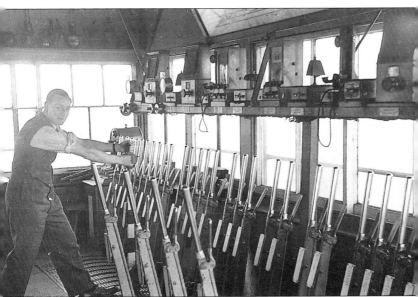

Eventually the block shelf was used to accommodate signal repeaters, lamp repeaters, track circuit repeaters and telephones. Today, a traditional block shelf can support everything from additional control panels for signals and level crossings, to Rules & Regulations folders and potted plants.

F. THE WORKING ENVIRONMENT

The unique combination of electrical and mechanical equipment that constituted the traditional signalbox produced a unique breed of men (and latterly women) to operate it, to bring it to life. *(Picture 95)* A signalman's job was both physical and mental, requiring not just the observance and repetition of procedures, Rules & Regulations, but also initiative and reasoned decision-making when required. It could be argued that one of the reasons signalboxes became the accepted means of controlling the movement of trains in the 1870s was because it was then that better educated and more skilled working men were available to operate them. In the 1850s the magazine *Punch* caricatured 'pointsmen' and other railway staff as incompetent. In the 1870s, signalmen were respected men in society, with a considerable pride in the responsibility of their work.

This pride was manifest not just in the way the job was carried out, but the way in which the equipment and the whole operating floor environment within a signalbox was maintained. Over the years, many signalmen tended this area with as much care as they would their Victorian front parlours. Regular men at signalboxes would often divide the tasks between them, and allocate particular areas for cleaning. The tops of levers and the brasses on the instrumentation would be kept bright. Windows were cleaned regularly inside and out, and when linoleum began to find its way into boxes, this was also polished to a very high shine. There must have been signalboxes all over the country where this was not the case, as it would have been particularly difficult to keep up appearances in busy signalboxes. But judging from the well-worn but polished condition of many block instruments that have survived from all parts of the country, standards must have been genuinely high.

Below (95a):
Neilsons Sidings, Wellingborough, photographed in June 1987 and closed six months later. *Author*

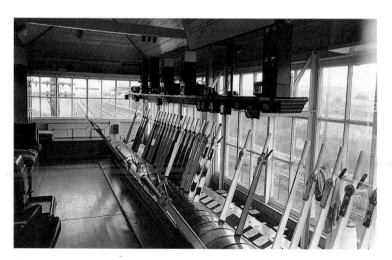

Over the last 10 years, hundreds of mechanical signalboxes have closed, the majority having been demolished. Sometimes individual boxes have become redundant due to a reduction of traffic or the loss of a siding or yard, and sometimes groups of boxes have closed due to the upgrading of whole lines with the installation of continuous track circuiting and colour light signals controlled from new signalling centres. The scale of the losses may surprise many railway enthusiasts more familiar with statistics for the scrapping of locomotives and rolling stock. It might be said that no other building type in this country is so under threat. Today many high street buildings that were once built for a specific purpose, such as post offices or banks, become redundant, but few are simply demolished. Most find alternative uses; signalboxes do not.

To list all closures over the last 10 years would be tedious, so the following is a summary of the major losses. As it is, it makes depressing reading for enthusiasts and architectural historians alike.

1986
This year witnessed completion of electrification to Norwich and the improvements included a new, but temporary, signalling centre opened in the city on 8 June. Traditional mechanical signalboxes which were abolished included:

Below (96):
Trowse Lower Junction (GE7).
Robert Humm Collection

Norwich Thorpe Passenger Yard	1-2 February
Norwich Thorpe Junction	13 July
Trowse Upper Junction	21 September
Trowse Lower Junction	30 November *(Picture 96)*

(The panel box itself closed on 15 March the following year when the area came under the control of Colchester powerbox.)

For enthusiasts, the most emotive closures during 1986 were the result of the 'Leicester Gap' resignalling scheme. The scheme was so named because the last remaining stretch of the former Midland main line controlled by mechanical signalboxes and semaphores passed through Leicester. Resignalling with multi-aspect colour light signals had been achieved on this route as far south as Loughborough in 1969 when Trent powerbox opened that year, and northwards from St Pancras as far as Irchester South by 1979, when that ex-MR box became the fringe to West Hampstead. Construction of a new signalling centre on the site of the former MPD at Leicester began in 1984, and on 29 June 1986 a dozen mechanical signalboxes closed in the first phase of the resignalling scheme:

| Bell Lane (Leicester) |
| Desford Colliery Sidings |
| Kibworth Station |
| Kilby Bridge |
| Knighton South Junction |
| Leicester North |
| Little Bowden Junction |
| London Road Junction (Leicester) |
| Market Harborough (No 3) |
| Wigston North Junction |
| Wigston South Junction |
| Wistow |

This left four mechanical boxes north of Leicester, and semaphores controlling trains through Kettering and Wellingborough.

1987
The remainder of the 'Leicester Gap' scheme was finally completed in 1987 in two further stages. On 12 April the boxes north of Leicester were closed:

| Loughborough |
| Sileby |
| Syston North Junction (Picture 97) |
| Syston South Junction |

And then on 5-6 December, the last mechanical signalboxes on the Midland main line finally succumbed:

| Finedon Road (Wellingborough) |
| Glendon North Junction |
| Irchester South |
| Kettering Junction |
| Kettering Station |
| Neilsons Sidings (Wellingborough) |
| Wellingborough Station (Picture 98) |

Below (97):
Syston North Junction (MR3a), photographed in April 1984. *Author*

Opposite top (98):
Wellingborough Station signalbox on 3 October 1987 with No 45121 passing on an up parcels. The new colour light signals are all ready for use. *Author*

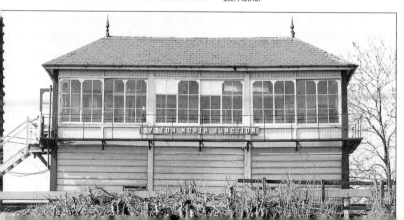

On the Southern Region a new box opened on 11 July 1987 at Oxted with a panel to take over the work of East Grinstead, Hurst Green Junction, Lingfield and Oxted Station mechanical signalboxes.

In former Great Western Railway territory, the area controlled from Exeter powerbox (opened 1 April 1985) was extended in two further stages during 1987. On 21-23 March 1987 Silk Mill Crossing and Taunton East Junction (147 levers) closed. The latter had housed a temporary panel since its neighbour, the 135-lever Taunton West Station signalbox, closed in May the previous year. Between 2–4 May, Newton Abbot East and West boxes (206 and 153 levers respectively) were taken out of use, followed on 8 November by the much smaller 74-lever signalbox at Totnes. *(Pictures 99 & 100)*

Below (99):
The impressive all-timber 206-lever Newton Abbot East signalbox, photographed in July 1985. *Author*

1988

During 1988 the largest number of closures were due to the introduction of Radio Electronic Token Block (RETB) in Scotland and Wales.

In the first few months of the year, Banavie box *(Picture 101)* began to supervise the line to Fort William once controlled from the mechanical signalboxes at:

Ardui
Arrochar & Tarbet
Bridge of Orchy
Corrour
Crianlarich Upper
Dalmally
Garelochhead
Glen Douglas
Rannoch
Spean Bridge
Taynuilt
Tulloch *(Picture 102)*
Tyndrum Upper

Barmouth South
Caersws
Dovey Junction
Harlech
Newton
Porthmadog
Talerddig
Tywyn
Welshpool
Westbury

Later during July, Dingwall North and South boxes closed and RETB supervised from Inverness box led to the closure of Muir of Ord signalbox on 21 August 1988.

Between 21 and 23 September RETB between Sutton Bridge Junction, Shrewsbury and Machynlleth (supervised from the latter), led to the closure of the following mechanical boxes:

Above (100):
Totnes signalbox, photographed in August 1978. *G. Scott-Lowe*

Opposite above (101):
The former West Highland Extension signalbox at Banavie, photographed with its new replacement in June 1986. A sympathetic renewal. *M. E. Haddon*

Opposite centre (102):
Tulloch was a typical example of the platform-level signalbox on the West Highland line of the NBR. Photographed in April 1958. *Photomatic*

Opposite below (103):
Goring-by-Sea, an example of the LB&SCR's new turn-of-the-century design. Photographed in August 1969. *J. Scrace*

At the opposite end of the country, a new panel in Lancing signalbox took over the work of the following mechanical signalboxes on the Southern Region during

Angmering
Goring-by-Sea *(Picture 103)*
Portslade
Shoreham-by-Sea 'A'
Shoreham-by-Sea 'B'
West Worthing
Worthing

May and June 1988:

1989

1989 witnessed the replacement of significant installations of postwar signalling technology at York and at Liverpool Street, London. *(Picture 104)* The late 1980s booming economy encouraged some massive building schemes in the capital, including the redevelopment of Liverpool Street and Broad Street station sites. As part of this work, Liverpool Street was equipped with a new Integrated Electronic Control Centre (IECC) and between 24 March and 2 April 1989 the postwar Liverpool Street and Bethnal Green signalboxes were taken out of use.

But the event that received the most attention was the commissioning of the new IECC at York to replace the impressive 1951 OCS (one control switch) panel. As with the latter installation, remodelling of the station layout was a major part of the new scheme, work starting during September 1988 and ending early in 1989. Temporary panels were installed in a number of signalboxes outside the city, and then on 11 May 1989 the 1951 panel along with Yard South, Yard North and Skelton Junction was decommissioned and over the next few days the new panel was brought into use. It was not fully operational until 10 September 1989, when control of colour light signals on the Selby Diversion was transferred from a smaller panel that had been in use only since September 1983. The new layouts are lean and efficient, and the new signalling centre is completely anonymous and self-effacing. There could be no more stark a contrast to the elaborate webs of NER track and the highly visible and massive signalcabins of a previous more assured generation.

Another major scheme started to take shape during 1989 in Scotland. In July, just to

the west of Glasgow, the first stage of Yoker IECC was commissioned and Clydebank Dock Junction, Dalmuir Park, High Street Junction, Hyndland and Singer signalboxes were closed. Over the next few years more boxes were abolished as the area of control was extended. To complete the story, in October 1990 Milngavie and Westerton signalboxes were closed, followed by Airdrie, Bellgrove, Heatheryknowe, Parkhead North Junction, Shettleston and Sunnyside Junction in 1991, and in February 1992 Bowling, Craigendoran and Dumbarton succumbed.

1990

The last London terminus traditionally controlled by semaphores and the absolute block system was finally resignalled in 1990. In April that year, Marylebone IECC was commissioned and the following signalboxes

Great Missenden	23 April
Northolt Junction East	28-29 May
Sudbury Hill	29 May
High Wycombe South	10 August
Gerrards Cross	11-13 August
West Ruislip	11-13 August

Opposite (104):
Liverpool Street signalbox, photographed when new in 1949. *BR/Topical*

Above (105):
Nos 31203 and 31199 passing the 50-lever, 1885, LNWR Lichfield City signalbox on 4 January 1989. *Author*

Left (106):
The ex-MS&LR signalbox at Friargate Crossing, Grimsby, photographed in June 1990 just two months after it was accidentally burnt out. *Author*

73

were abolished:

On a smaller scale the extension of the panel at Oxted to control the Uckfield line led to the closure of Crowborough, Eridge and Hever signalboxes at the beginning of the year. The significance of this event was not so much the loss of the signalbox structures, but that it marked the final extinction from active service of Tyers one-wire, two-position semaphore block instruments, some of the first successful electrical instruments from the early years of block signalling and used on the LB&SCR since the 1870s. (Uckfield signalbox finally closed on 12 May 1991.)

1991

In 1991 the commissioning of a new signalling centre on Tyneside lead to the closure of Benton, Darlington, Gateshead, Heaton, Newcastle and Tyne Yard signalboxes, and in July Northampton's Nos 1, 3 and 4 signalboxes closed, control passing to Rugby powerbox.

1992

In April 1992, the oasis of semaphores around Ely disappeared when Dock Junction, North and North Junction signalboxes were abolished and control transferred to the Cambridge panel. Semaphores also disappeared from Lichfield when the City box was closed in October, *(Picture 105)* colour light signals replacing semaphores at Trent Valley Junction as well.

1993

Upgrading of London's suburban signalling continued in 1993 when the new IECC at Ashford (Kent) was opened in February. Chislehurst Junction, Orpington and Sevenoaks, built during the Southern Region's late 1950s and early 1960s resignalling scheme, closed as a result.

Above (107):
Wellowgate, Grimsby. Opened at the beginning of the 1880s, and photographed here over 100 years later in November 1990. *Author*

During September, another 1960s box, Pasture Street in Grimsby, took over the control of the station there and level crossings formally supervised by Garden Street, Wellowgate, Friargate Crossing and Littlefield Crossing. Friargate box had been burnt out on 12 April 1990, over three years before the new signalling was complete. *(Picture 106)* All were of 1880s vintage with original MS&LR lever frames and traditional single-needle GCR and GNR-type block instruments and bells. Wellowgate has since found a new home at the NRM. *(Picture 107)*

1994

The effect of the Clapham disaster of December 1988, the economic slump of the early 1990s, and the entrenchment leading up to rail privatisation obviously slowed the pace of major resignalling projects as witnessed by the above statistics. However, if the first few years of the new decade saw few major losses of signalboxes, then 1994 made up for the apparent lull in modernisation. That year saw the commissioning of two important signalling schemes in Yorkshire and Merseyside which led to a major cull of traditional mechanical signalboxes. Both projects were aimed at improving local train services and, looking at them completely objectively, these improvements were long overdue.

In February, Merseyrail opened its new signalling centre at Sandhills in the midst of Liverpool's dock wasteland as part of a major investment to improve inner city, cross-Mersey and outer suburban services. For the traveller the investment has been well worth it, but the following list gives some idea of what, from a railway enthusiast's perspective, had to be sacrificed:

Name	Opened	Closed
Ainsdale	1878	11 March
Aughton Road (G)	1928	11 March
Bidston Dee Junction	1936	18 September
Bidston East Junction	1937	10 September
Birkdale	1905	11 March *(Picture 108)*
Birkenhead Central	1886	10 September
Birkenhead North No1	1888	10 September
Birkenhead North No2	1888	10 September
Bootle Junction	1986	11 March
Brook Hall Road (G)	1885	11 March
Duke Street	1921	11 March
Eccles Crossing	1912	11 March *(Picture 109)*
Freshfield (G)	1878	1 May
Hall Road	1878	15 May
Hightown	1878	11 March
Hoylake	1889	18 September
James Street	1977	18 September
Leasowe (G)	1938	21 August
Maghull	1875	10 February
Moreton	1932	18 September
New Brighton	1888	18 September
Rock Ferry	1957	18 September
Southport	1917	20 March
Town Green	1940s	10 February
Walton Junction	1903	10 February
Waterloo	1881	11 March
West Kirby	1932	18 September

Southport signalbox had been the pride of the L&YR when the company resignalled the station in 1917 with electro-pneumatically operated semaphores and points controlled from a 87-miniature lever Westinghouse K power frame. *(Picture 110)*

Across the Pennines, in Yorkshire a similar rationalisation was taking place in an effort to improve services. In November, Leeds took over control of the remaining mechanically-signalled former MR lines, and the following signalboxes were the casualties of the new efficient electrified railway that emerged:

Top (108):
The L&YR's signalbox at Birkdale in May 1996, still intact two years after closure. *Author*

Left (109).
The standard brick-based L&YR signalbox at Eccles Crossing, Formby, on a wet November day in 1989. *Author*

Right (110):
The operating floor of Southport powerbox, photographed in 1936. *Real Photographs, E1082*

Name	Opened	Closed
Apperley Junction	1927	4 July
Bingley Station	1932	22 October
Cononley	1964	22 October
Guiseley	1906	11 July
Guiseley Junction	1901	25 July
Ilkley Junction	1913	11 July
Keighley Station Junction	1884	22 October
Kildwick	1895	22 October
Kirkstall Junction	1910	4 July
Shipley Bingley Junction	1907	25 July
Shipley Bradford Junction	1903	25 July
Skipton Station North	1915	22 October
Skipton Station South	1906	22 October *(Picture 111)*

1995

At the end of 1994, modernisation turned its face southwards to the LT&SR when in September Upminster IECC opened. This led to the closure between April and July 1995 of signalboxes at Barking, Laindon, Leigh-on-Sea, Shoeburyness, Southend Central and Upminster.

1996

During 1996 the area of Upminster control was extended further and in April 1996 West Thurrock Junction, Grays, Tilbury Riverside, Low Street and Pitsea signalboxes closed. When Ripple Lane, Dagenham Dock,

Rainham and Purfleet signalboxes were closed the following month, the Upminster resignalling was complete.

THE FUTURE

At the time of writing (1997), rationalisation continues to threaten individual boxes up and down the country. A number of schemes are already in hand and/or are planned to be implemented by the time this book appears in print.

The last phase of GE resignalling is nearing completion between Manor Park and Ilford station, with an extension of Colchester powerbox's control through

Marks Tey, Witham, Chelmsford and Ingatestone in the near future. On Railtrack South West, steady progress is being made with resignalling between Wimbledon and Eastleigh. Barnes powerbox (1959) will close, its area controlled by a new panel in Wimbledon powerbox; Woking (1937) and Surbiton (1970) powerboxes will close and a new panel at Woking will take over their functions. On Railtrack LNE, it was made public at the end of 1996 that by the end of the century, 62 manual signalboxes in its area will have been abolished with the loss of up to 217 jobs. As part of this scheme it is planned that by early 1997, Worksop East and West, Shireoaks East Junction, Shireoaks Station, Brancliffe East Junction and Dinnington will all have closed.

Left (111):
Skipton Station South signalbox, photographed in April 1984, 10 years before closure. *Author*

Below (112):
The CR's signalbox at Broughty Ferry on the Dundee & Arbroath Joint line, photographed in May 1993. This box closed on 31 July 1995 and is now listed Grade A. *Author*

As the previous chapter clearly shows, the number of signalboxes on the national network is declining all the time. *(Picture 113)* With the results of privatisation still not certain, it is difficult to predict how long the remainder will last. Some observers believe that eventually there will be more signalboxes in preservation than controlling the former British Rail network.

At the end of 1996, there were 617 signalboxes built by the pre-Grouping (1923) companies still controlling trains on the national network. The figures make an interesting comparison to those companies' official statistics at the time of grouping:

Railway Company	1996	Grouping
Barry Rly	2	39
Cambrian Rly	1	92
CLC	5	128
CR	26	666
FR	16	69
G&SWR	9	286
GCR	21	510 (including MS&LR)
GER	55	650
GNR	35	603
GNoSR	6	127
GWR	56	1,646
HR	10	154
L&SWR	16	531
L&YR	37	752
LB&SCR	21	349
LC&DR	1	145
LNWR	78	1,254
LNWR/C&H	2	(included in LNWR figures)
LNW&GWJt	9	(probably included in LNWR figures)
LT&SR	1	(included in MR figures)
M&CR	1	29
M&GNR	1	90
MR	46	1,203
MS&LR	21	(included in GCR figures)
NBR	17	641
NER	94	1,191
NLR	4	not known
NSR	8	146
SER	11	270
SE&CR	4	415 (including SER & LC&DR figures)
TVR	4	118

Many interesting, unusual and typical signalboxes have been lost in that time. *(Picture 114)* There are, of course, many places all over the country, from Scotland to Cornwall and from Wales to East Anglia, where trains are still controlled from mechanical signalboxes with semaphore signals — Norfolk and Cumbria are singled out for special attention below. But there are now few 'centres' of traditional signalling. Of those that still remain, three have been selected as places where you can still appreciate what mechanical signalling was once all about.

EX-GER SIGNALBOXES

The ex-GER lines in Norfolk are still a pleasure to visit. On the route between

Peterborough and Norwich, traditional heavy wooden crossing gates still protect the public level crossings where traditional signalboxes and mechanical equipment can be studied at close quarters without trespassing. *(Picture 115)* Almost everything functions as originally intended, although being completely objective, this must indicate a lack of capital to undertake modernisation. When the author photographed Attleborough station and platform-mounted signalbox, it was bedecked with potted plants, the staff and volunteers obviously still proud to have won a best-kept station award in 1992. *(Picture 116)* Other local signalboxes at Eccles Road, Harling Road and Thetford *(Picture 117)*, to single out just a few, all appeared well looked after. This made the contrast with Shippea Hill signalbox all the greater. What vestige of paint remained was of LNER vintage and, still leaning backwards on temporary timber props as it has done for many years, it seems in a precarious state to be the fringe box to Cambridge powerbox. *(Picture 118)*

SIGNALBOXES IN CUMBRIA

The ex-FR lines also provide some interesting contrasts. Those signalboxes with stone bases are fine buildings that even the non-railway enthusiast can appreciate. St Bees sits comfortably and in complete harmony with the well-maintained buildings of the station and the village it serves. *(Picture 119)* At the bottom of the box steps, ivy has been trained up the side of what would otherwise have been the only unsightly modern addition — the Portaloo. Other boxes such as Bootle and Askam literally blend into their surroundings, their stone bases imaginatively extended to form part of the station platform perimeter walls. *(Picture 120)* Elsewhere the FR built in brick and timber, good examples surviving at Millom and Foxfield. At Foxfield the signalbox and waiting room are combined, the exterior of the solid wooden structure enhanced within the last few years by the use of a green and cream livery. *(Picture 121)*

But not all is so well manicured in Cumbria and inappropriate repairs have degraded a number of signalboxes. The roof of the ex-FR box at Millom, for example, has been covered with felt in place of slate tiles *(Picture 122)*, and the same cheap and expedient formula has been used for the ex-LNWR Workington Main No 3, and Bransty No 1 at Whitehaven.

Opposite above (113):
LNWR's Heaton Norris Junction No 2 being dismantled. In the background is the new Heaton Norris Junction signalbox which opened in March 1955. *BR(LMR)*

Opposite (114):
Portobello East signalbox, straddling the lines on the outskirts of Edinburgh, was opened by the NBR on 26 September 1909 with a 94-lever frame. It closed on 6 May 1973. *Eric Treacy*

Right (115):
Eccles Road receiving attention from the S&T department on 23 June 1996. *Author*

Above (116):
Attleborough station
and signalbox
photographed on
23 June 1996 *Author*

Right (117):
Thetford signalbox;
23 June 1996. *Author*

Opposite above (118):
Shippea Hill, fringe
signalbox to
Cambridge powerbox,
photographed on the
same day. *Author*

Opposite (119):
St Bees signalbox and
station, photographed
in May 1996. *Author*

SHROPSHIRE

The lines radiating from Shrewsbury still boast a clutch of mechanical signalboxes. To the east, the route to Wolverhampton is controlled by five mechanical boxes; northwards to Crewe there are also five; and northwest to Wrexham there are just two.

The most interesting line, from a signalling perspective, runs south from Shrewsbury into Herefordshire and South Wales. Just south of the town is Sutton Bridge Junction signalbox. *(Picture 123)* Built to GWR specifications in 1913 with 61 levers, it controlled junctions to the Severn Valley Railway and the line to Welshpool and Aberystwyth. The main line southwards to Abergavenny is now one of the few long stretches of double track still operated by the block system. The line as far as Hereford was formerly jointly controlled by the GWR and the LNWR (as was Shrewsbury station) and the signalboxes on this stretch were built to neither company's standard design. There are manual signalboxes at Dorrington, Church Stretton (currently permanently switched out), Marshbrook, Craven Arms, Onibury, Bromfield, Woofferton Junction, Leominster, *(Picture 124)* Moreton-on-Lugg, Hereford, *(Picture 125)* Tram Inn and Pontrilas. *(Picture 126)*

At Shrewsbury itself, there are six mechanical signalboxes within walking distance of the town centre: Harlescott Crossing, *(Picture 127)* Crewe Bank, Crewe Junction, Severn Bridge Junction, Sutton Bridge Junction and Abbey Foregate. Of these, Severn Bridge Junction has the accolade of being the largest mechanical signalbox in the country with 180 levers still worked by two signalmen per shift. Built in 1903 to the LNWR's distinctive modular design (Type 4), the structure is set in the triangle of tracks to the south of the station. *(Picture 128)* The box still works absolute block to its neighbours — Abbey Foregate on the Wolverhampton line — Sutton Bridge

Opposite above (120):
Bootle signalbox and station, photographed in May 1996 *Author*

Opposite (121):
Foxfield signalbox and attached waiting room; May 1996. *Author*

Above (122):
Millom signalbox photographed in May 1996. *Author*

Above (123):
Sutton Bridge
Junction signalbox,
Shrewsbury,
photographed in
September
1996. *Author*

Right (124):
The distinctive
LNW&GWJt Rly
1870s-style signalbox
at Leominster,
photographed in
January 1996. The
length of many of
these boxes was
almost the same as
their width. *Author*

Opposite above (125):
The attractive
LNW&GWJt Rly
Type 2 signalbox at
Hereford (Ayleston
Hill), photographed
in June 1996. *Author*

Opposite (126):
McKenzie & Holland
design of signalbox
at Pontrilas,
photographed in
December
1986. *Author*

87

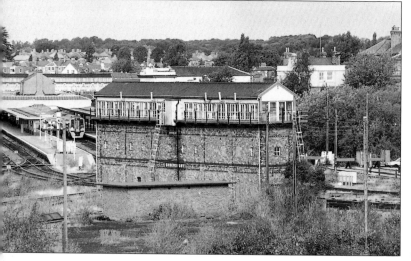

Top (127):
Harlescott Crossing on the LNWR's route between Shrewsbury and Crewe clearly shows signs of having been sympathetically extended to twice its original length at some time. Photographed in June 1996. *Author*

Above (128):
Severn Bridge Junction, Shrewsbury, the largest operational mechanical signalbox in the country. Photographed in September 1996. *Author*

Opposite above (129):
Crewe Junction signalbox, Shrewsbury, photographed on the same day as Severn Bridge junction. *Author*

Opposite (130).
At track level, the locking room of Crewe Junction signalbox stands barely two storeys high. This photograph of the back of the box, taken in September 1996, shows how the structure is built against the viaduct at the northern end of the station. *Author*

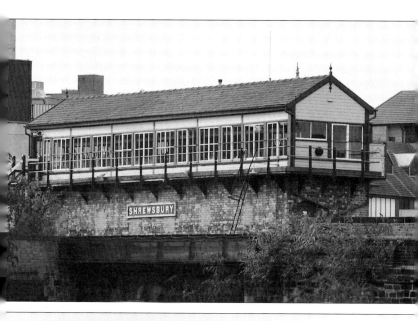

Junction on the Hereford/Newport/Cardiff route (both standard GWR boxes) — and Crewe Junction to the north of the station.

Crewe Junction controls the northern end of the station, and like Severn Bridge Junction was built to the LNWR's current standard when the station was considerably enlarged at the beginning of the 20th century. Crewe Junction is another large box with 120 levers but is single-manned. *(Pictures 129 & 130)* It protects the junction of the ex-GWR route from Chester and Wrexham and the former LNWR line coming in from Crewe. It was on this junction on 5 October 1907, when the box was only four years old, that 4-6-0 No 2052 *Stephenson* hurtled off the Crewe line at high speed, the ensuing pile-up claiming 18 lives.

Undoubtedly, it is the equipment and operating practices within these two substantial LNWR signalboxes which make Shrewsbury an important mechanical signalling centre, some might say museum. But unfortunately, not many people are able to experience their unique atmosphere (although a commercial video was made showing some of the work inside Severn Bridge Junction in 1990), so most enthusiasts have to be content with the dwindling number of GWR lower quadrant semaphores

in and around the station. There used to be more, but rationalisation has taken its toll and during the past few years standard upper quadrants and colour light signals have appeared. For example, until 1988, there was an impressive iron gantry outside Abbey Foregate signalbox dating from the commissioning of the new box in 1914. *(Picture 131)* The five wooden signal posts it supported, complete with seven ex-GWR lower quadrant arms, lasted until the end.

LINCOLNSHIRE

A few decades ago, major stations were the places to see mechanical signalling really earning its maintenance costs, but now only Worcester, Stirling, Shrewsbury and Lincoln are operated in a traditional way. There are still four mechanical signalboxes within the

Above (131):
Abbey Foregate signalbox on the left with Severn Bridge Junction in the background, photographed on 20 April 1987. *Author*

Opposite (132):
Lincoln Central station in August 1990, looking west. High Street and East Holmes signalboxes are in the background. *Author*

city of Lincoln following considerable rationalisation in 1985. Pelham Street, to the east of the station, is the largest box with a frame of 100 levers installed in the existing GNR signalbox in 1918. Protecting the western end of the station and the busy main road into the city, is High Street signalbox. Though the timber crossing gates were replaced by barriers within the last few years, it is still worth standing on High Street to watch Lincoln's best signalmen coping with road traffic, throngs of pedestrians and departing trains with the minimum of delay. A few hundred yards further west is East Holmes signalbox which once controlled entry to Lincoln's extensive sidings next to Brayford Pool, now the site of the city's brand-new university. *(Picture 132)* At the westernmost extremity of this former yard stands West Holmes signalbox built as part of the GN&GEJt Railway Committee's work in 1882.

Interesting though the selection of signalboxes is that have been mentioned so far, they control today very little traffic compared with the situation a century ago.

Hardly any shunting takes place and the boxes contain many white (spare) levers, so although much original equipment survives, there is little sense of what traditional signalling was once capable of. The best, and probably only, place to appreciate mechanical signalling operating to its limits and still keeping a large amount of traffic moving on the national network is centred around Barnetby in North Lincolnshire. This is former MS&LR territory where the lines from Grimsby and Immingham join at Ulceby and Brocklesby junctions before branching off into three routes at Wrawby Junction. The original route goes through Gainsborough to Retford and Sheffield, and the other two slightly later lines go to Scunthorpe and Doncaster, Market Rasen and Lincoln.

The area is a little oasis of mainly mechanical signalling surrounded by encroaching panel boxes. On the Gainsborough-Brigg line there are still manual signalboxes at Gainsborough Central, Northorpe, Kirton Lime Sidings and Brigg. But to the northwest Scunthorpe powerbox (1973) fringes to Appleby; to the south

Holton-le-Moor signalbox has had a panel since April 1989; and in Grimsby, the area controlled from Pasture Street panel box was extended through the town to Marsh Junction in August 1993. Within those boundaries the surviving mechanical signalboxes are to be found at Marsh Junction, Great Coates No 1, Pyewipe, Stallingborough, Roxton Sidings, Ulceby Junction, Goxhill, Barrow Road, Oxmarsh Crossing, Brocklesby Junction, *(Picture 133)* Barnetby East, Wrawby Junction and Elsham. There are also power frames at Immingham East Junction, Immingham Reception Sidings (both dating back to GCR days) and a panel in Immingham West Junction.

The largest signalbox is Wrawby Junction (Class D) boasting 137 levers, *(Picture 134)* followed in size by Brocklesby Junction (Class B) with 96 and Barnetby East (Class B) with 72 levers. The frames in all three signalboxes were manufactured by McKenzie & Holland with distinctive GCR 'jug handles' in front of the lever tops instead of the more common catch handles behind. In Barnetby East, apart from colour light distant signals and two Intermediate Block Signals, the physical effort of moving points and signals is as great as it was when the box opened in 1914. *(Picture 135)* By comparison, Wrawby

Junction with its frame at the back of the box, has had some motor-operated points for over a decade now, easing the signalman's job. Nevertheless, with the up and down signals traditionally grouped at opposite ends of the frame, the signalman expends his energy continually walking to and fro during a shift.

Undoubtedly the busiest stretch of line is between Brocklesby Junction, Barnetby East and Wrawby Junction. Standing on Barnetby station there is hardly a quiet moment as oil trains pass to and from the Immingham refineries, whilst iron-ore trains ply between Immingham docks and Scunthorpe steelworks, passing trains of imported coal. *(Picture 136)* Between Barnetby East and Wrawby Junction there are up and down fast

Below (133):
Brocklesby Junction in July 1990. *Author*

Opposite above (134):
The 137-lever Wrawby Junction signalbox, photographed in July 1990. *Author*

Opposite below (135):
4-6-0 No 44767 *George Stephenson* passing Barnetby East on 20 May 1995 with the first steam working in this area since the 1960s. *Author*

93

Above (136):
Nos 37275 *Stainless Pioneer* and 37106 passing Wrawby Junction and heading east towards Barnetby with empty iron-ore wagons on 8 June 1990. *Author*

lines, up and down slow lines and a down goods. Both slow lines used to continue from Barnetby to Brocklesby Junction, until they were taken out of use at the end of 1987. With the added pressure on line capacity of imported coal coming from Immingham, the down slow had to be reinstated in March 1995 and it now sees frequent use. All traffic between Wrawby Junction and Barnetby East is dealt with under absolute block regulations and signalled by semaphores, and from there to Brocklesby Junction there are IBSs on both the down fast (main) and down slow lines.

Apart from the diesel-hauled trains, the area might seem caught in a time-warp to the enthusiast. But for those keeping the traditional equipment functioning, modern working practices since privatisation have seen an end to the traditional and long-established British Rail and LNER system. The provision of three regular signalmen for each box and various grades of relief for rest days etc, and their 8hr shift patterns of 2pm–10pm, 10pm–6am, 6am–2pm officially ended in October 1994. Since then the shift hours have been 00.01–08.00, 08.01–16.00, 16.01–23.59. There are now four regular men for each box, rotating round a roster where once

every four weeks a man covers relief work instead of a regular shift. At the time of writing, there are 76 regular signalmen in the area and 20 relief signalmen, most having six to eight designated 'core boxes' to cover. To maintain all the mechanical and electrical equipment there is a small local S&T team, but any specialist locking jobs are the responsibility of one man based in Leeds. His nearest support is in Birmingham.

As well as traditional equipment within the signalboxes, there are over 100 paraffin lamps to illuminate semaphore and ground signals. These have to been changed every week with freshly trimmed and filled replacements, a job currently undertaken by two lampmen based at Grimsby who are also expected to cover the lines north of the Humber as far as Scarborough.

It is difficult to predict how long this pocket of busy mechanical signalling will last. At the very end of the 1980s, signalling along the Wrawby Junction to Lincoln line was concentrated in just three signalboxes with new electronic panels leading to the closure of five manual boxes. During 1993, the area of control of Pasture Street panel box in Grimsby was extended westwards towards Brocklesby, and its area is due to be increased in the near future. Sooner or later, Wrawby Junction and Barnetby East and the art of mechanical signalling will disappear, and what was once commonplace will be consigned to memory, photographs and perhaps video.

The preservation of signalboxes is a recent phenomenon. By the 1870s the Victorians were building signalboxes of some architectural merit and obviously building them to last. They were, however, quite prepared to demolish and replace quite substantial structures when necessary, not afraid to upgrade (when the funds were available) if the new buildings and track layouts were, in their opinion, better both functionally and aesthetically than those they replaced. This was most obvious at large provincial centres and at London termini. For example, in the space of 30 years between 1867 and the turn of the century, Waterloo terminus of the L&SWR saw the erection, extension and demolition of three huge mechanical signalboxes. Crewe North Junction signalbox with 144 levers built in 1878, was demolished and replaced in 1906 by an equally impressive structure to house a frame of 266 miniature levers of Webb & Thompson patent 'All Electric Signalling' design. This in turn was partly demolished in the early years of World War 2, so that a less vulnerable signalbox could be constructed over the remains of its base. *(Picture 137)* This structure is currently preserved as part of the Crewe Heritage Centre.

Replacement before signalboxes were life-expired was not confined to large stations. By 1900, it is believed that the majority of the MR's first standard signalboxes built in the 1870s all over the system had been replaced. Even the GNR, which extended rather than rebuilt, had by the new century pulled down many of its 1870s signalboxes when widening its main line. *(Picture 138)*

This lack of sentimentality for old structures continued between the two World Wars. The SR demolished many boxes along its newly electrified main lines during the 1930s without any protests. After World War 2, and particularly following the Modernisation Report of 1955, British Railways would have swept away all mechanical signalboxes if it had had the resources. *(Picture 139)* Only lack of capital investment kept the majority of traditional signalboxes open.

Below (137):
Crewe North Junction and the base of its 1906 predecessor, photographed in August 1984. The box closed on 19 July the following year. *Author*

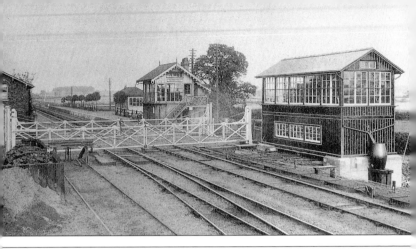

Top (138):
Tempsford station on the GNR main line showing
the original 1870s signalbox and its replacement
ready for the extension of the goods line in the
mid-1890s. *Transport Trust Library*

Above (139):
Almost the end for the CLC signalbox at Stockport,
Tiviot Dale, in 1968, as '8F' 2-8-0 No 48551 trundles
past with a westbound freight. *R. Elsdon*

Opposite above (140):
Shireoaks station signalbox in the 1960s. *Robert
Humm Collection*

Opposite (141):
Shireoaks station signalbox in September
1987. *Author*

SIGNALBOXES ON THE NATIONAL NETWORK

Preservation in a fundamental sense can simply mean survival, and for structures and equipment to survive they have to be maintained. For signalboxes still in use on the national network, maintenance is still the best way of ensuring preservation. Having said that, preservation for an architectural historian also implies maintaining the original appearance of a structure. From what evidence there is, both pre-Grouping and the 'big four' companies appear to have carried out repair work, and most noticeably, extensions to signalboxes, with a respect for the original style of architecture, even if it was not fashionable at the time. The GWR sympathetically enlarged certain boxes, and a number of ex-GNR signalboxes on the main line were extended by the LNER, the new work matching very closely the existing. The ex-LNWR Harlescott signalbox outside Shrewsbury *(see Picture 127)* has been extended to twice its original length at some time, though to the casual observer the extension is difficult to detect. There are numerous other examples.

These types of modifications, of course, may have been the cheapest option at the time, and were not necessarily carried out with any overt intentions towards architectural integrity. But for whatever reasons, the results were more sympathetic than much of British Rail's maintenance and repair work has been in the last few decades.

The type and arrangement of windows is one of the most characteristic features of all signalboxes, and yet this aspect appears to have been treated with the least regard when repairs were necessary. Compare Shireoaks Station (MS&LR) before and after modification, for example.*(Pictures 140 & 141)* Now look at the former GNR signalboxes at St James Deeping and St Nicholas Deeping only a few miles apart on the line between Peterborough and Spalding. Both structures, though different in size, would have looked the same, but the latter has had its windows replaced with what are from an architectural point of view totally inappropriate new ones. *(Pictures 142 & 143)* Those responsible might argue that safety, visibility and cost were involved in the decision-making, but obviously these factors led to two completely different solutions at Ranskill and Grove Road on the East Coast main line when both ex-GNR signalboxes there, now housing signalling panels, had to be fitted with new windows. *(Pictures 144 & 145)* The manager responsible for Ranskill should be applauded.

At Mouldsworth Junction (CLC) recent major repair work has also included the fitting of replacement windows unlike the originals, but more fundamental has been the insertion of completely new brickwork to replace the original timber base. The work has been done to a high standard, and it is good to see bricks laid to other than stretcher bond, but historically, apart from the roof and lever frame, Mouldsworth Junction is really a new structure. *(Picture 146)*

As a business, Railtrack can argue that it cannot be expected to be interested in preservation *per se*. In purely business terms, a building like any other piece of equipment has to play some part in earning revenue. Unfortunately it has never been that simple because, like it or not, British Rail has until recently owned a considerable proportion of what we now consider as the nation's heritage, something valued other than in purely monetary terms. Many railway buildings and structures were constructed to impress, and many were, and still are, of considerable architectural merit. Because of this, many have been given statutory protection since World War 2 through the Listing system, now the responsibility of English Heritage. This places restrictions on modifications and demolition. Listing structures has been and is perceived by many managers of British Rail and Railtrack as adding to the problems of running a modern railway.

If permission to demolish is not granted, adaptive reuse is often the best solution if a building is no longer needed for its original purpose. But there is one fundamental problem with this in relation to many railway properties. Most are next to railway lines, and railway lines can be noisy and dangerous places. Both these factors can deter potential new owners. Station buildings are usually separated from the track by at least the width of a platform, and so many have successfully passed into private ownership as homes or industrial units. But signalboxes are invariably situated only feet from the running lines and consequently it has proved almost impossible to find new uses for the majority of them.

The story of preserving redundant signalboxes *in situ* on British Rail is consequently an unsatisfactory one. Broadly speaking, regardless of whether a structure is listed or not, if it is not in revenue-earning service, and it cannot be adapted for alternative uses, it suffers neglect and invariably dereliction. St Albans South signalbox is the most embarrassing example of this. Closed as an operational signalbox in 1979, and listed by English Heritage, it has remained *in situ* but unused, a target for graffiti artists and vandals. *(Picture 147)* In

Below (147):
Ex-MR (Type 2b) St Albans South signalbox in March 1988 surrounded by the paraphernalia of another age. *John C. Baker*

Above (148):
4-6-0 No 73135 passing ex-MR California Crossing signalbox just south of Gloucester with a Paignton–Bradford train on 12 August 1959. *S. Rickard*

Left (149):
The same signalbox beautifully restored at Toddington. Photographed in October 1993. *Author*

this case demolition ought to be considered acceptable, especially as so many former MR signalboxes still survive, and those on preserved railways like the Midland Railway Trust are accessible to the public.

This form of preservation, by moving redundant signalboxes to other locations, is a solution that has proved successful, but which has meant a rather flexible interpretation of the laws governing listed buildings. At Stamford, Robert Humm & Co has moved the former MR signalbox a few hundred yards from its original site to just next to the station buildings and the firm's main bookshop. At Brooksby, between Leicester and Melton Mowbray, another ex-MR signalbox became a cricket pavilion, but that was unusual. There are other odd examples, but undoubtedly the best solution to date has been to sell signalboxes to preservation societies where they can still function as originally intended. *(Pictures 148 & 149)*

SIGNALBOXES ON PRESERVED LINES

Today, no preserved railway is considered complete without semaphores and signalboxes, but this was not true in their early days. Then, signalling took second place to the restoration of locomotives and the running of trains under 'one engine in steam' regulations. Inevitably attitudes changed as it was realised that good signalling practices could increase the number of engines and trains pulling fare-paying tourists. The story of signalling on the Severn Valley Railway is an interesting example of the progress made in this area of preservation.

As on so many other preserved lines, signalboxes had been demolished by a retreating British Rail. The first signalbox to be rebuilt was at Bridgnorth during 1968/9 with the wooden superstructure from Pensnett signalbox and the majority of the 30-lever frame from Windmill End box. At the next station south — Hampton Loade — the signalbox superstructure was rescued just in time, *(Picture 150)* but the original frame was lost and a new one had to be fitted. This came from Ledbury North End signalbox. As the preserved railway extended its operations southwards, Arley was one of the

stations that had to be resignalled. There a standard LNWR box from Yorton, just north of Shrewsbury, which had closed on 15 April 1973, was erected during 1976 and equipped with a 26-lever frame (with six spaces) from Kidderminster Station. At Highley and Bewdley the signalboxes had fortunately passed intact into SVR hands, but all needed a considerable amount of restoration work. By the 1980s, if the enthusiast wanted to see an authentically run branch line complete with genuine signalling, then the Severn Valley Railway was the place to see it.

Having demonstrated that it was possible for volunteers to restore and maintain complex signalling installations, it is not surprising that the idea to preserve a really large mechanical signalbox came from within the ranks of the Severn Valley Railway's S&T Department. By the mid-1980s, there were many small to medium sized signalboxes on preserved lines up and down the country, numerous lever frames and other equipment in the NRM, but no representative large mechanical box in preservation. In locomotive terms it was as though nothing bigger than 2-6-0s survived — no Pacifics — no '9Fs'.

To redress the balance, the former GWR's Exeter West signalbox was targeted for preservation. It was the ideal candidate in a number of ways. It was certainly large, containing 131 levers, but it looked comparatively easy to dismantle as it had been built in manageable prefabricated wooden sections. It was also due to close in 1985 during the Great Western's 150th birthday celebrations, and this timing could only increase the chances of a successful preservation attempt. *(Picture 151)*

Opposite above (150):
The McKenzie & Holland signalbox at Hampton Loade on the Severn Valley Railway, photographed during the 1992 season. *John Powell*

Opposite (151):
Exeter West signalbox, rebuilt at the Crewe Heritage Centre. When Exeter St David's station was reconstructed just before World War 1, the box was originally meant to be a temporary structure. *Author*

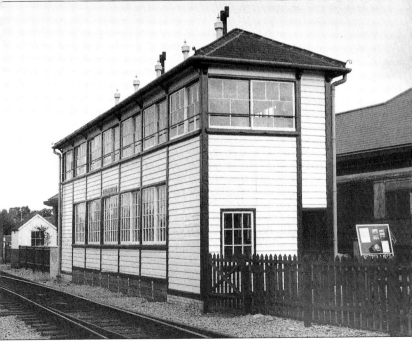

British Rail in Exeter proved particularly helpful and after months of preparation, a team of dedicated signalling enthusiasts descended on Exeter West signalbox during the summer of 1985 and after a late night/early morning line occupation on 13/14 July, had the structure neatly disassembled into kit form ready for re-erection elsewhere. It was some years before the box could be rebuilt, but now Exeter West is beautifully restored after many hours of work by a dedicated few, fully operational and on show to the public at the Crewe Heritage Centre. *(Picture 152)* In 1995 it won the Westinghouse Signalling Award section of the Ian Allan National Railway Heritage Awards. It is by far the best readily accessible example of what mechanical signalling was all about in its heyday.

Exeter West is likely to remain the largest mechanical signalbox in preservation, but since the mid-1980s the size of signalboxes being privately preserved has certainly increased. On 21/22 November 1987, the Severn Valley Railway successfully commissioned a brand-new brick-based GW Type 7d signalbox at Kidderminster, complete with a 62-lever frame (including eight spaces). *(Pictures 153 & 154)* Every

Above (152):
The 131-lever frame inside Exeter West. It was fitted in April 1959, replacing the original 114-lever frame, dismantled in 1985, and refitted by a few dedicated volunteers starting in 1991. These photographs were both taken in the summer of 1993. *Author*

detail is to the highest standard of workmanship, and it provides a fitting conclusion to the story of SVR signalling.

When the former MR signalboxes at Kilby Bridge (near Leicester) and Kettering station were closed in 1986 and 87 respectively, both were saved by the Midland Railway Trust and moved to its line in Derbyshire. Kilby Bridge, complete with its 32-lever MR tumbler frame, was re-erected at Hammersmith, the western end of the line, and Kettering station, with its 44-lever MR tappet frame, was resited prominently and accessibly at Swanwick Junction during 1988. The latter is another impressive large mechanical box worth a visit. *(Picture 155)*

No doubt other large signalbox projects are being planned, but to finish this chapter we turn to the Great Central Railway based at Loughborough. Nearing completion at Swithland Sidings, almost in the centre of the

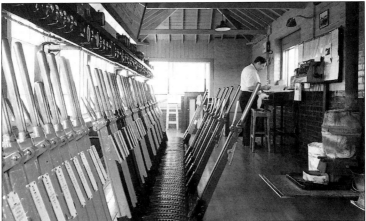

preserved railway, is a GCR Type 5 signalbox, the superstructure from Aylesbury South erected on a new brick base supporting a 55-lever GW vertical tappet frame. *(Picture 156)* When finished, it is planned that the signalbox will control not only two loops, but also up and down through lines on which trains will be controlled using the block system. If this is achieved, then a very important piece of active signalling preservation history will be made.

Top (153):
The Severn Valley Railway's Kidderminster station signalbox, photographed in July 1996. *Author*

Above (154):
Half the size of Exeter West's frame, the interior of the Kidderminster box is still impressive. *Author*

LISTED SIGNALBOXES

The following signalboxes, in use on the national network, currently out of use or in private preservation, are listed by English Heritage, Cadw — Welsh Historic Monuments, and Historic Scotland, Historic Buildings List, as worthy of preservation. The name, status and identity numbers have been supplied from the official records maintained by the National Monuments Record Centre, Swindon, Cadw, Cardiff and Historic Scotland, Edinburgh. In England and Wales buildings are graded with numbers, for example Grade II, in Scotland they are graded with letters, for example Grade C(S). The dates and details of design have been added from Peter Kay's Signal Box Directory.

Above (155):
Swanwick Junction signalbox, formerly Kettering station (MR Type 4c), photographed at its new home in May 1990. *Author*

Right (156):
The new Swithland sidings signalbox on the Great Central Railway, photographed in September 1996. *Author*

Signalbox Name	Design	Date	Listed Status	Number
Aiskew	NEnk	nk	Grade II	435689
Appleby	RSCo	1885	Grade II	165974
Arisaig	RSCo	1901	Grade B	HB326
Askam	Furness 2	1890	Grade II	388443
Athelney	GW27c	1906	delisted	271221
Barmouth South	Dutton 1	1890	GradeII	5204
Beckingham	GN1	1877	Grade II	241096
Beverley	NES4	1911	Grade II	167169
Birmingham New Street	BR(LMR)PB	1966	Grade II	442131
Boat of Garten North	McK&H3	1885	Grade B	HB258
Brocklesby Junction	GC5	1914	Grade II	431839
Broughty Ferry	Cal N1	1887	Grade A	HB25823
Burton Agnes	NES1b	1875	Grade II	167791
Burton Agnes	NES1a	1903	Grade II	167793
Butterley (Ais Gill)	Mid2b	1900	Grade II	79121
Caersws	Dutton 1	1891	Grade II	8698
Canterbury West	overhead	1928	Grade II	444443
Carnforth Station Junc	Furness 4	1903	Grade II	181825
Chappel & Wakes Colne	GE7	1891	Grade II	421981
Chathill	NEN1	c1873	Grade II	409553
Crawley	S&F5	1877	Grade II	363395
Crediton	LSW1	1875	Grade II	387107
Dunragit	LMS 12	1927	Grade C(S)	16766
Ecclesfield West	Mid2b	1896	Grade II	382379
Elsham	RSCo	1885	Grade II	165920
Embsay Station	Mid4d	1923	Grade II	323930
Errol	Cal N1	1877	Grade B	HB11603
Falgrave (Scarborough)	NES4	1908	Grade II	447780
Feock	Chasewater Rly	nk	Grade II	63306
Gorse Hill Bridges	nk	nk	Grade II	317922
Grand Sluice (Boston)	GN1	1874	Grade II	191748
Hale	nk	nk	Grade II	212882
Haltwhistle	NEn/s	nk	Grade II	240761
Hammersmith (Kilby Bridge)	Mid3b	1900	Grade II	352001
Heckington	GN1	1877	Grade II	192604
Helmsdale South	Dutton 1	1894	Grade B	HB7184
Hexham	NEN5 overhead	1918	Grade II	239247
Holywell Junction	LNW4	1902	Grade II	511
Howden	NES1a	1873	Grade II	408831
Instow	LSW1	1870s	Grade II	98792
Keighley Station Junc	Mid2a	1884	Grade II	338098
Kingussie	McK&H3	nk	Grade B	HB36282
Kippen	NB n/s	1893	Grade B	HB8181
Kirkham Abbey	NES1a	1873	Grade II	329558
Kirton Lime Sidings	RSCo	1886	Grade II	439164
Knareborough	NEn/s	1873	Grade II	430811
Knockando	GNoS 1	1899	Grade C(S)	HB8502
Llandrindod Wells	LNW4	1876	Grade II	9357
Llangollen Station	GW7a	1898	Grade II	1084
Mostyn	LNW4	1902	Grade II	597

Signalbox Name	Design	Date	Listed Status	Number
Murthly	(HR)	nk	Grade B	HB43644
Nafferton	NEnk	nk	Grade II	166966
Nairn West and East	McK&H3	1891	Grade B	HB38455
New Bridge	NES1a	1876	Grade II	440545
Norham	NEN4	nk	Grade II	237946
Oakham Level Crossing	Mid2b	1899	Grade II	435875
Oswestry	Dutton2	1892	Grade II	255565
Pantyffynnon South	GW5	1892	Grade II	14813
Parbold	S&F9	1877	Grade II	357858
Plumpton	LB&SC2b	1891	Grade II	416120
Pontypridd Junction	TVR	1907	Grade II	13527
Princes Risborough	GW7b	1907	Grade II	46480
Rhyl No.1	LNW4	1900	Grade II	1515
Rhyl No.2	LNW4	1900	Grade II	1514
Sandford	GWnk	nk	Grade II	33292
Selside	Mid4a	1907	Grade II	355233
Shrewsbury Crewe Junc	LNW4	1903	Grade II	456427
Shrewsbury Severn Bridge Junction	LNW4	1903	Grade II	454643
Sleaford East	GN1	1882	Grade II	191907
St Albans South	Mid2a	1892	Grade II	163511
St Mary's Crossing	GW2	1870s	Grade II	133156
Stoke Canon	S&F4	1874	Grade II	86133
Stow Park	GN1	1877	Grade II	197088
Sudbury	NS1	1885	Grade II	273915
Swanwick Junction (Kettering Station)	Mid4c	1913	delisted	230122
Swinderby	Mid3a	1901	Grade II	192150
Topsham	LSW1	1870s	Grade II	420554
Torquay	GWn/s	1876	Grade II	390767
Ty Croes	LNW/C&H	1871	Grade II	5733
Wansford	LNW5	1907	Grade II	414074
Warmley	Mid4a	1918	Grade II	406621
Weaverthorpe	NES1a	1873	Grade II	329413
West Street Junction (Boston)	GN1	1874	Grade II	191746
Weston-super-Mare	Bristol & Exeter Rly	1866	Grade II	33266
Williton	Bristol & Exeter Rly	1875	Grade II	265027
Woking	SR13	1937	Grade II	428087
Wolferton	GE5	1884	Grade II*	222165
Worksop East	MS&L2	1880	Grade II	241356
Wrawby Junction	GC5	1916	Grade II	431308
Wylam	NEN5 overhead	1897	Grade II	239532

KEY

(G)	gatebox, usually a former signalbox no longer used for controlling trains
(E)	emergency or irregular use only
(EBP)	emergency block post
(NBP)	not a block post
(OOU)	out of use but not officially abolished
(RR)	former signalbox reduced to relay room
E	original signalbox structure extended at some later date
GF or gf	ground frame
IECC	integrated electronic control centre
OA&GB	Oldham, Ashton-under-Lyne & Guide Bridge
PB	powerbox
PR	panel room, other than powerboxes and ex-manual signalboxes since fitted with panels
RETB	radio electronic token block
SB & BO	signalbox and booking office
SCC	signalling control centre
nk	information not known
n/s	non-standard
u	opening date of signalbox may not be accurate

Signalbox Name	Company	Date	Design	Mechanical or Panel	No of Levers	Date of Frame or Panel
Abbey Foregate	GWR	1914	GW7d	lever frame	93	1914
Aberbeeg Junction	GWR	1892	GW5	lever frame	65	1914
Abercynon	GWR	1932	GW27c s/h	lever frame & panels	35	1932 & 77 & 89
Aberdeen	BR(ScR)	1981	BR(ScR)PB	panel		1981
Abergavenny	GWR	1934	GW28b	lever frame	52	1934
Abergele	LNWR	1902	LNW4	lever frame	60	1902
Aberthaw	Barry Rly	1897	Barry 2	lever frame	53	1962
Acle	GER	1883	GE3/S&F	lever frame	20	1883
Acton Canal Wharf	MR	1895	Mid2b	lever frame	35	1965
Acton Lane SF (NBP)	BR(LMR)	1964	BR(LMR)15	lever frame	30	1964
Acton Wells Junction	NLR	1892	NL3a	panel		1990
Aldershot	L&SWR	c1900	LSW4	lever frame	24	c1900
Allerton Junction	BR(LMR)	1960	BR(LMR)15	lever frame	70	1960
Allington Junction	GNR	1875	GN1	lever frame	22	1882
Alnmouth	NER	1907	NE N3	panel		1990
Alrewas	LNWR	1899	LNW4	panel		1982
Alstone Crossing (G)	MR	1891	Mid2a	panel		1982
Altofts Junction	BR(ER)	1990	BR(ER)RR	panel s/h		1990
Amberley	SR	1934	SR BO extension	lever frame	14	1934
Ancaster	GNR	u1873	GN1	lever frame	30	1887
Annan	G&SWR	1876	GSW1	lever frame	20	1973
Annat (G)	BR(ScR)	1963	BR(ScR) n/s	lever frame	16	1963
Appleby (Lincs)	MS&LR	1885	RSCo	lever frame	23	1885
Appleby North	BR(LMR)	1951	LMS11c	lever frame	25	1951
Appleford Crossing (G)	BR(WR)	1952	GW14	none		
Arbroath North	NBR	1911	NB7	lever frame	72	1911
Archcliffe Junction	SR	1928	SR11a	lever frame	40	1928
Arnside	FR	nk	Furness4	lever frame	35	1957
Arpley Junction	LNWR	1918	LNW5	lever frame	54	1918
Arundel	SR	1938	SR13	panel		1979

Signalbox Name	Company	Date	Design	Mechanical or Panel	No of Levers	Date of Frame or Panel
Ascott-under-Wychwood	GWR	1883	GW4b	lever frame	25	1949
Ash Crossing	BR(SR)	1966	BR(SR)18	panel		1966
Ash Vale Junction	LSWR	1879	LSW n/s	panel		1984
Ashburys	GCR	1906	GC5	panel		1984
Ashford IECC	BR(SR)	1993	-	VDUs, etc		1993
Ashington (OOU)	NER	1896	NE N1	lever frame	25	1938
Ashton Junction	GWR	1906	GW27c	lever frame	49	1906
Ashton Moss North Junction	L&YR	1911	L&Y	lever frame	56	1911
Ashton OA&GB Junction	BR(LMR)	1965	BR(LMR)15	lever frame	40	1965
Ashwell	MR	1912	Mid4a	lever frame	25	1958
Askam	FR	1890	Furness 2	lever frame	22	1890
Aspatria	M&CR	1891	M&C	lever frame	25	1940
Astley	BR(LMR)	1972	BR(LMR)15 s/h	lever frame	15	1972
Aston SCC	BR(LMR)	1957	BR(LMR)15	lever fram & panel	20	1992
Atherton Goods Yard	BR(LMR)	1956	BR(LMR)15	lever frame	35	1956
Attleborough	GER	1883	GE4/McK&H	lever frame	36	1912
Auchterarder	CR	1895	Cal N2	lever frame	16	1895
Aviemore	HR	1898	McK&H3/HR	lever frame & panel	30	1971 & 79
Awre (G,E)	GWR	1909	GW7d	none		
Aylesford	SR	1921	SR11a	lever frame	26	1921
Baguley Fold Junction	L&YR	1890	RSCo	lever frame	32	1890
Balne (G)	BR(NER)	1957	BR(NER)17	lever frame	5	1957
Bamber Bridge Station (G)	L&YR	1906	L&Y	none		
Banavie	BR(ScR)	1987	BR(ScR) n/s	RETB		1987
Banbury North	GWR	1900	GW7b	lever frame	95	1957
Banbury South	GWR	1908	GW7d	lever frame & panel	87	1944 & 92
Bangor	LMSR	1923	LNW5	lever frame	60	1923
Bardon Hill	MR	1899	Mid2b	panel		nk
Bardon Mill	NER	1874	NE N1	lever frame	20	1966
Bare Lane	LMSR	1937	LMS11c	lever frame	32	1937
Bargoed	BR(WR)	1970	BR(WR)37b s/h	lever frame	51	1970 s/h
Barking	BR(ER)	1961	BR(ER)PB	panel		1961
Barkston East Junction	GNR	1882	GN1	lever frame	29	1882
Barlaston (G)	BR(LMR)	1985	Portakabin	panel		1985
Barlby (G)	NER	1898	NE S1a	lever frame	7	1932
Barnby (G)	BR(ER)	1977	BR(ER)20	panel		1977
Barnby Moor & Sutton (G,E)	GNR	1872	GN1	none		
Barnes	SR	1959	BR(SR)17PB	panel		1959
Barnetby East	GCR	1914	GC5	lever frame	72	1914
Barnham	LB&SCR	1911	LBSC3b	lever frame	75	1911
Barnhill	CR	u1874	Cal N1	lever frame	20	nk
Barnsley Station	L&YR	1901	L&Y	lever frame	56	1901
Barrhead	CR	1894	Cal54	lever frame	25	1973
Barrhill	LMSR	1935	GSW7	lever frame	18	1935
Barrow-in-Furness	FR	1907	Furness 4	lever frame	67	1907
Barrow Road Crossing (G)	MS&LR	1885	RSCo	lever frame	8	1885
Barry	Barry Rly	1897	Barry1	lever frame	77	1957
Barry Island (OOU)	GWR	1930	McK&H3	lever frame	23	1930
Barry West	NBR	1908	NB7	panel		1995
Barton Hill	LNER	1936	LNER13	lever frame	16	1936
Baschurch	GWR	1880	McK&H3	lever frame	25	1911
Basford Hall Junction	LNWR	1897	LNW4	lever frame	70	1897
Basingstoke	BR(SR)	1966	BR(SR)19PB	panel		1966
Bathley Lane (G)	LNER	1930	GN4b	panel		1976
Batley	LNWR	1878	LNW4	panel		1966
Bearley West Junction	GWR	1907	GW7d	lever frame	30	1974

Signalbox Name	Company	Date	Design	Mechanical or Panel	No of Levers	Date of Frame or Panel
Beckingham	GNR	1877	GN1	panel		1977
Bedale	NER	1875	NE S1a	lever frame	31	1909
Bedford St Johns No1	BR(LMR)	1977	BR(LMR)15	lever frame	50	1911
Bedlington North	NER	1912	NE N4	lever frame	60	1912
Bedlington South	NER	nk	NE N1	lever frame	30	1940
Beeston Castle & Tarporley	LNWR	1915	LNW5	lever frame	26	1915
Beighton Station	GCR	nk	GC n/s	lever frame	49	1962
Belasis Lane	LNER	1929	NE S4	lever frame	25	1929
Bellwater Junction	GNR	1913	GN4a	lever frame	25	1913
Belmont (G)	NER	1914	NE S5	lever frame	5	1965
Bentley Heath Crossing (G)	GWR	1932	GW28b	lever frame	49	1932
Berwick	LB&SCR	1879	S&F5	lever frame	17	1879
Bescot Down Tower	BR(LMR)	1965	BR(LMR)PB	panel		1965
Bescot Up Hump (NBP)	BR(LMR)	1963	BR(LMR)15	lever frame	20	1963
Bestwood Park Junction	BR(LMR)	1951	BR(LMR)14	lever frame	55	1951
Betley Road	LNWR	1875	LNW3	lever frame	22	1904
Betteshanger Colliery (OOU)	SR	1923	SR11a	lever frame	16	1923
Beverley Station	NER	1911	NE S4	lever frame	20	1911
Bexhill	LB&SCR	1876	S&F	lever frame	19	1876
Billingham	NER	1904	NE C2a	lever frame	50	1945
Billinghurst	LB&SCR	u1876	S&F1b	lever frame	19	1876
Bingham	GNR	1875E	GN1	lever frame	40	1922
Birkdale	L&YR	1905	L&Y hipped	none		
Birmingham New Street	BR(LMR)	1966	BR(LMR)PB	panel		1966
Bishop's Stortford South	LNER	1931	LNER11b	lever frame & panel	45	1931 & 60
Bishton Crossing GF (G)	GWR	1941	GW12a	lever frame	3	1941
Blackford	LMSR	1933	LMS12	lever frame	25	1933
Blackpool North No1	BR(LMR)	1959	BR(LMR)15	lever frame	65	1959
Blackpool North No2	L&YR	1896	L&Y	lever frame	80	1896
Blackrod Junction	L&YR	1879	GWCo	lever frame	37	1890
Blair Atholl	HR	u1890	McK&H3/HR	lever frame	18	1969
Blakedown	GWR	1888	GW4c	panel	-	1980
Blankney	LNER	1928	GN4b	lever frame	30	1928
Blaydon	NER	n/k E	NE N2	lever frame	43	1929
Blea Moor	LMSR	1941	LMS11c	lever frame	30	1941
Bletchley	BR(LMR)	1965	BR(LMR)PB	panel	-	1965
Blotoft	GER	1882	GE2	lever frame	16	1882
Bloxwich	BR(LMR)	1959	BR(LMR)15	lever frame	30	1959
Bognor Regis	SR	1938	SR13	lever frame	66	1938
Boldon Colliery	NER	1893	NE N1	panel	-	1985
Bollo Lane Junction	L&SWR	1878	LSW2	panel	-	1983
Bootle	FR	1874	Furness 1	lever frame	14	1977
Bopeep Junction	SER	c1912	SE	lever frame	24	1973
Boston Dock Swing Bridge (G)	GNR	(by)1887	Boston Corporation	lever frame	12	1913
Bottesford West Junction	GNR	1876	GN1	lever frame	38	1876
Bournemouth	SR	1928	SR n/s	lever frame	60	1928
Bournemouth Carriage Sidings GF (NBP)	L&SWR	1888	LSW3a	lever frame	14	1888
Bowesfield	NER	1905	NE n/s	lever frame & panel	36	1905 & 69
Bradwell Sidings	NSR	1889	NS2	lever frame	35	1969
Brampton Fell	NER	u1918	NE N4	lever frame	20	u1918
Brancliffe East Junction	GCR	1905	GC5	lever frame	25	1905
Brandon	LNER	1931	LNER11c	lever frame	40	1931
Branksome	L&SWR	1886	LSW3a	lever frame	30	1886
Bransty	LNWR	1899	LNW4	lever frame	60	1899

Signalbox Name	Company	Date	Design	Mechanical or Panel	No of Levers	Date of Frame or Panel
Brereton Sidings	LNWR	1908	LNW5	lever frame	20	1908
Brewery Sidings	L&YR	1894	L&Y	lever frame	45	1894
Bridlington South	NER	1875E	NE S1a	lever frame	65	1912
Brierfield Station (G)	L&LR	1876	S&F8	panel		1986
Brigg	MS&LR	1885	RSCo	lever frame	30	1923
Brightside (E)	BR(ER)	1965	BR(ER) n/s	panel		u1965
Brimsdown	LNER	1944	GE7	lever frame & panel	37	u1902 & 88
Bristol	BR(WR)	1970	BR(WR)PB	panel		1970
Brockenhurst	BR(SR)	1964	BR(SR)18	panel		1978
Brocklesby Junction	GCR	1914	GC5	lever frame	96	1914
Bromfield	LNW&GWJt	1873	LNW&GWJt 1	lever frame	29	1956
Bromley Cross (G)	L&YR	1875	Yardley 1	lever frame	16	1902
Broomfleet	NER	1904	NE S2	lever frame	60	1904
Brough East	NER	1904	NE S2	lever frame	52	1904
Broxbourne	BR(ER)	1960	BR(ER)18PB	panel		1960
Brundall	GER	1883	GE 3/Stevens	lever frame	35	1927
Burscough Bridge Junction	L&YR	1922	L&Y	panel		1993
Bury St Edmunds Yard	GER	1888	GE7/McK&H	lever frame	53	1888
Buxton	LNWR	1894	LNW4	lever frame	45	1894
Cadder	NBR	1901	NB4	panel		1971
Caersws (G)	Cambrian	1891	Dutton 1	lever frame	18	1891
Caldicot Crossing GF (G, NBP)	BR(WR)	1979	BR(WR) Hut	gf & panel	10	1979
Cambridge	BR(ER)	1982	BR(ER)PB	panel		1982
Camden Road Junction	NLR	1896	NL3b	panel		1987
Canning Street North	LNWR	1900	LNW4	lever frame	18	1900
Canterbury East	SE&CR	c1911	SEC	lever frame	28	c1911
Canterbury West	SR	1928	overhead	lever frame	72	1928
Cantley	GER	1887	GE7	lever frame	22	1913
Cardiff	BR(WR)	1966	BR(WR) PB	panel		1966
Cark	BR(LMR)	1952	LMS11b s/h	lever frame	30	1952
Carleton Crossing	LMSR	1924	LNW5	lever frame	12	1924
Carlisle	BR(LMR)	1973	BR(LMR)PB	panel		1973
Carlton (G, EBP)	BR(ER)	1977	BR(ER)20	panel		1977
Carmarthen Junction	BR(WR)	1956	BR(WR)16a	panel		1985
Carmont	CR	1876	Cal N1	lever frame	18	1907
Carmuirs East Junction	NBR	1882	NB4	lever frame	28	u1901
Carmuirs West Junction	CR	1882	Cal n/s	lever frame	20	1912
Carnforth East Junction	MR	1902	Mid3a	lever frame	24	1902
Carnforth F&M Junction	FR	1896	Furness 4	lever frame	66	1896
Carnforth Station Junction	FR	1903	Furness 4	lever frame	59	1903
Carnoustie	CR	1898	Cal N2	lever frame	20	1984
Carterhouse Junction	LNWR	1896	LNW4	lever frame	30	1896
Castleford Gates	NER	1882E	NE S1	lever frame	32	1927
Castleford Station	NER	1882	NE S1	lever frame & panel	40	1914 & 73
Castleton East Junction	BR(LMR)	1963	BR(LMR)15	lever frame	65	1963
Cathcart	BR(ScR)	1961	BR(ScR)PB	panel		1961
Cattal	NER	nk	NE S5	lever frame	15	1934
Cave (G)	NER	1904	NE S4	lever frame	16	1904
Caverswall	LMSR	1942	LMS11c	lever frame	35	1942
Cayton (G)	NER	1908	NE S4	lever frame	14	1908
Cemetery North	NER	1905	NE C2a	lever frame	20	1955
Chapel-en-le-Frith	BR(LMR)	1957	BR(LMR)15	lever frame	20	1957
Chard Junction	BR(WR)	1982	BR(WR) n/s	panel		1982
Charlton Lane Crossing (G)	SER	1894	S&F12a	lever frame	7	1894
Chartham	SER	1880s	SE	lever frame	22	1880s

Signalbox Name	Company	Date	Design	Mechanical or Panel	No of Levers	Date of Frame or Panel
Cheadle Hulme	LNWR	1901	LNW4	lever frame	36	1901
Cheetham Hill Junction	L&YR	1890	L&Y	lever frame	60	1890
Chelford Frame (NBP)	BR(LMR)	1959	BR(LMR) n/s	lever frame	20	1959
Chelmsford	GER	1899	GE7	lever frame & panel	45	1899 & 1961
Cheshunt Junction	GER	1891	GE8	panel		1975
Chester	BR(LMR)	1984	BR(LMR)PB	panel		1984
Chichester	LB&SCR	1882	S&F5	panel		1991
Chingford	GER	1920	GE7	lever frame & panel	30	1958 & 60
Chinley	BR(LMR)	1980	BR(LMR)15	panel		1982
Chippenham Junction	LNER	u1925	GE7	lever frame	16	u1925
Chorley (G, E)	L&YR	1879	GWCo	lever frame	4	1920
Christ's Hospital	LB&SCR	1902	LBSC3b	lever frame	36	1902
Church Fenton	NER	1904	NE S3	lever frame		1968
Church Stretton (OOU)	LNW&GWJt	1872	LNW&GWJt 1	lever frame	25	nk
Clachnaharry (NBP)	HR	1890s	McK&H3/HR	lever frame	4	1912
Clacton	GER	1891	GE7	lever frame	52	1891
Clarbeston Road	GWR	1906	GW7c	panel		1988
Clarence Road	NER	1904	NE n/s	lever frame	36	1932
Claypole (G, EBP)	BR(ER)	1977	BR(ER)20	panel		1977
Cliff House	BR(NER)	1958	BR(NER)17	lever frame & panel	70	1958 & 61
Clipstone West Junction	GCR	1917	GC5	lever frame & panel	37	1917 & 86
Codsall	GWR	1929	GW28	lever frame	25	1929
Colchester	BR(ER)	1983	BR(ER)PB	panel		1983
Collingham (E)	MR	1901	Mid3a	none		
Collyhurst Street	?	1894	RSCo s/h	lever frame	56	1894
Colthorp Siding (G)	GWR	1912	GW7c	gf & panel	2	1978
Colwich	BR(LMR)	1961	BR(LMR)15	lever frame & panel	30	1961 & 74
Corby Gates	BR(NER)	1955	BR(NER)17	lever frame	26	1955
Corkickle No1	BR(LMR)	1958	BR(LMR)15	lever frame	65	1958
Corkickle No2	BR(LMR)	1958	BR(LMR)15	lever frame	35	1958
Cosford	GWR	1939	GW12	lever frame	39	1939
Cottage Lane Crossing (E)	LMSR	1927	Mid4d	none		
Coundon Road Station	LNWR	1876	LNW4	lever frame	23	1876
Coventry	BR(LMR)	1962	BR(LMR)PB	panel		nk
Cowbridge Road	BR(WR)	1965	BR(WR) Hut	panel		u1965
Cowlairs	BR(ScR)	1956	BR(ScR)16c	panels		1956 & 80
Crabley Creek	NER	1891E	NE S1b	lever frame	12	1956
Crag Hall	NER	1878	NE C1	lever frame	30	1906
Craigo	CR	1877	Cal N1	lever frame	21	1907
Craven Arms Crossing	GWR	nk	GW34	lever frame	30	nk
Crediton	L&SWR	1875	LSW1	panel		1984
Crewe Coal Yard	LMSR	1939	LMS13	lever frame	65	1939
Crewe Signalling Centre	BR(LMR)	1985	BR(LMR)PB	panel		1985
Crewe Sort Sidings North	BR(LMR)	1962	BR(LMR)15	panel		1962
Crewe Steel Works	LMSR	1935	LMS11c	lever frame	20	1935
Cricklewood Depot (NBP)	BR(LMR)	1979	BR(LMR)PB	panel		1979
Crigglestone Junction	L&YR	1901	L&Y	lever frame	32	1901
Croes Newydd North Fork	GWR	1905E	GW27c	lever frame	83	1940
Croft Sidings	LNWR	1901	LNW4	lever frame	30	1901
Cromer	M&GNR	1920	M&GN n/s	lever frame	35	1954
Crosfields Crossing	LNWR	1913	LNW4	lever frame	18	1913
Crow Nest Junction	BR(LMR)	1972	BR(LMR)15	lever frame	25	1972
Culgaith	MR	1908	Mid4a	lever frame	16	1908
Cumbernauld	CR	1870s	Cal n/s	lever frame	35	1911
Cupar	NBR	nk	NB7	lever frame	32	nk
Curzon Street (RR)	BR(LMR)	1966	BR(LMR)15			

Signalbox Name	Company	Date	Design	Mechanical or Panel	No of Levers	Date of Frame or Panel
Cutsyke Junction	BR(ER)	1975	BR(ER) n/s	panel		1975
Cuxton	SR	nk	SE	lever frame	29	nk
Daisyfield Station	L&YR	1873	S&F6	lever frame	16	1943
Dalton Junction	FR	1902	Furness 4	lever frame	20	1902
Dalwhinnie	HR	1909	Highland	lever frame	20	1966
Dartford	BR(SR)	1970	BR(SR)PB	panel		1970
Dawdon	NER	1905	NE N3	panel		1987
Deal	SR	1939	SR13	lever frame	42	1939
Deal Street	LMSR	1929	LMS n/s	power frame	80	1929
Deansgate Junction	BR(LMR)	1957	BR(LMR)15	panel		1991
Dee Marsh Junction	LNER	1930	GC5	lever frame	25	1930
Deganwy	LNWR	1914	LNW5	lever frame	18	1914
Denton Junction	LNWR	1888	LNW4	lever frame	18	1888
Derby	BR(LMR)	1969	BR(LMR)PB	panel		1969
Derby Road	GER	1891	GE7	lever frame	23	u1891
Diggle Junction	LNWR	1885	LNW4	lever frame	26	1885
Dinnington Colliery	GCR	1907	GC5	lever frame	29	1907
Dinting Station	GCR	1905	GC5	lever frame	43	1905
Disley	LNWR	1906	LNW4	lever frame	15	1906
Ditton Junction No1	BR(LMR)	1956	BR(LMR)15	lever frame	100	1956
Ditton Junction No2	BR(LMR)	1960	BR(LMR)15	lever frame	55	1960
Dodworth	BR(ER)	1959	BR(ER) n/s	lever frame	22	1959
Doncaster	BR(ER)	1979	BR(ER)PB	panel		1979
Dorchester	BR(SR)	1959	BR(SR)16	panel		1985
Dorking	SR	1938	SR13	lever frame	44	1938
Dorrington	LNW&GWJt	1872	LNW&GWJt 1	lever frame	33	1941
Dover Priory	SR	1930	SR12	panel		1980
Downham	GER	1881	GE2	lever frame	31	1881
Drakelow CEGB Sidings (NBP)	BR(LMR)	1969	BR(LMR)15	lever frame	25	1969
Driffield	NER	1875	NE S1a	lever frame & panel	3	1957 & 87
Drigg	FR	1874	Furness 1	lever frame	13	1882
Droitwich Spa	GWR	1907	GW7d	lever frame	79	1907
Dudding Hill Junction	MR	1902	Mid3a	lever frame	16	1902
Dullingham	GER	1883	GE4/Stevens	panel		1978
Dumfries	BR(ScR)	1957	BR(ScR)16c	lever frame & panels	28	1957
Dumfries South	BR(ScR)	1955	BR(ScR)16c	lever frame	32	1955
Dunblane	CR	1902	Cal N3	lever frame	60	1955
Dundee SC	BR(ScR)	1985	BR(ScR)PB	panel		1985
Dunkeld	HR	1919	Highland	lever frame	23	1919
Dunning	BR(ER)	1951	LNER15	lever frame	15	1951
Dunragit	LMSR	1927	LMS12	lever frame	34	1942
Dyce Junction	GNoSR	1880E	GNoS 1	lever frame	26	1928
Earles Sidings	LMS	1929	Mid4e	lever frame	35	1929
East Boldon	NER	1870s	NE N1	lever frame	26	1956
East Farleigh	SER	1892	SE	lever frame	25	1892
East Gate Junction	LNER	1924	LNER n/s	lever frame & panel	35	1924 & 83
East Holmes	GNR	u1873	GN1	lever frame	35	u1910
East Usk	BR(WR)	1961	BR(WR)37	lever frame	39	1961
Eastbourne	LB&SCR	1882	S&F5	panel		1991
Eastfield (NBP)	GNR	nk	GN1	lever frame	65	1893
Eastleigh	BR(SR)	1981	BR(SR)PB	panel		1981
Eastleigh (RR)	BR(SR)	1966	BR(SR)19PB			
Eastleigh DEMU Depot (NBP)	BR(SR)	1968	BR(SR)16	lever frame	24	1968
Eastleigh GF 'C' (NBP)	L&SWR	1918	LSW Hut	lever frame	29	u1918

Signalbox Name	Company	Date	Design	Mechanical or Panel	No of Levers	Date of Frame or Panel
Eccles	LMSR	1933	LMS11b	lever frame	60	1933
Eccles Road	GER	1883	GE4/McK&H	lever frame	21	1883
Ecclesfield West	MR	1896	Mid2b	panel		1979
Edale	MR	1893	Mid2b	lever frame	20	1893
Edge Hill	BR(LMR)	1961	BR(LMR)PB	panel		1985
Edgeley Junction No1	LNWR	1884	LNW4	lever frame	54	1884
Edgeley Junction No2	LNWR	1884	LNW4	lever frame	54	1884
Edinburgh SC	BR(ScR)	1976	BR(ScR)PB	panel		1976
Egginton Junction	NSR	1877	NS1	lever frame	14	1877
Elgin West	BR(ScR)	1951	Highland s/h	lever frame	26	1973
Elland	BR(NER)	1958	BR(NER)17	lever frame	60	1958
Ellesmere Port No4	BR(LMR)	1972	BR(LMR)15	lever frame	64	1924
Elmton & Cresswell	LMSR	1946	LMS11c	lever frame	48	1946
Elsham	MS&LR	1885	RSCo	lever frame	22	1885
Enfield Town	GER	1905	GE7	lever frame & panel	25	1959 & 60
Errol	CR	1877	Cal N1	lever frame	20	1911
Euston	BR(LMR)	1965	BR(LMR)PB	panel		1965
Everton (G)	BR(ER)	1976	BR(ER)20	panel		1976
Evesham	BR(WR)	1957	BR(WR)37a	lever frame	42	1957
Exeter	BR(WR)	1985	BR(WR)PB	panel		1985
Exmouth Junction	BR(SR)	1959	BR(SR)18	panel		1988
Falsgrave (Scarborough)	NER	1908	NE S4	lever frame	120	1908
Farncombe	L&SWR	1897	LSW4	panel		1986
Farnham	L&SWR	1901	LSW4	lever frame & panel	35	1901 & 85
Faversham	BR(SR)	1959	BR(SR)17PB	panel		1959
Felin Fran GF (NBP)	GWR	1913	GW27c	lever frame	56	1913
Felixstowe Beach	BR(ER)	1971	BR(ER) Hut	gf	15	1971
Felixstowe North Quay FD Shunting Pnl (NBP)	BR(ER)	1987		panel		1987
Feltham	BR(SR)	1974	BR(SR)PB	panel		1974
Feniton (G)	BR(WR)	1974	BR(WR)SB & BO	panel		1974
Fenny Compton	BR(WR)	1960	BR(WR)17	lever frame	77	1960
Fenny Stratford	LNWR	1883	LNW4	lever frame	22	1883
Ferme Park CC (NBP)	BR(ER)	1976	BR(ER) Hut	panel		1976
Ferrybridge	BR(NER)	1956	BR(NER)16b	panel		1981
Ferryhill	BR(NER)	1950	BR(NER)13	panel		1971
Ferryside	GWR	1880s	GW3	lever frame	24	1898
Fiddlers Ferry Power Station	BR(LMR)	1967	BR(LMR)15	lever frame	45	1967
Filey	NER	1911	NE S4	lever frame	24	1911
Finningley (G)	GNR	1877	GN1	panel		1977
Fiskerton (G)	MR	1902	Mid3a	lever frame	16	1902
Fiskerton Junction	LMSR	1929	Mid4e	lever frame	30	1929
Flag Lane (NBP)	BR(LMR)	1963	BR(LMR)15	lever frame	15	1963
Foley Crossing	NSR	1889	NS2	lever frame	37	1889
Folkestone Harbour	SR	1933	S&F5	lever frame	22	1933
Folkestone Junction	SR	1962	BR(SR)18PB	panel		1962
Folkestone West GF 'A' (NBP)	BR(SR)	1962	Hut	lever frame	10	1962
Forders Sidings	LMSR	1930	LMS11	lever frame	40	1930
Forest Gate Junction	GER	1893	GE7	lever frame & panel	19	1893 & 1949
Forres East	HR	1896	McK&H3/HR	lever frame	24	1967
Fort William	NBR	1894E	NB6b	lever frame & panel	30	1973 & 75
Fouldubs Junction	CR	1908	Cal N3	lever frame	40	1951
Foxfield	FR	1879E	Furness	lever frame	51	1909
Foxton (G)	GNR	1878	GN1	panel		1983
Fratton GF 'A' (NBP)	BR(SR)	1968	BR(SR)19 Hut	lever frame	24	1968

Signalbox Name	Company	Date	Design	Mechanical or Panel	No of Levers	Date of Frame or Panel
Freemans	BR(NER)	1956	BR(NER)16b	panel		1982
Frinton (G)	LNER	u1924	LNER Hut	gf	15	1936
Frisby Station	LMSR	1941	LMS11c	lever frame	10	1941
Frodsham Junction	LNWR	1912	LNW5	lever frame	32	1912
Furness Vale	LNWR	1887	LNW4	lever frame	22	1887
Gaerwen	LNWR	1882	LNW4	lever frame	20	1882
Gainsborough Central	MS&LR	1885	MS&L2	lever frame	26	1885
Gainsborough Lea Road	GNR	u1877	GN1	lever frame	36	1895
Gainsborough Trent Junction	BR(ER)	1964	BR(ER)19	lever frame	40	1964
Garnqueen North Junction	CR	nk	Cal S4	lever frame	40	1937
Garsdale (OOU)	MR	1910	Mid4c	lever frame	40	1910
Garston FL Frame (NBP)	BR(LMR)	1969	BR(LMR)15	lever frame	10	1969
Garston Junction	LNWR	1908	LNW5	lever frame	77	1908
Gartcosh Junction	CR	1899	Cal S4	lever frame	32	1899
Gartsherrie South Junction	CR	1903	Cal N3	lever frame	40	1977
Gascoigne Wood	NER	1908	NE S4	panel		1982
Gidea Park	LNER	1931	LNER11c	lever frame & panel	29	1931 & 49
Gilberdyke Junction	NER	1903	NE S2	lever frame	55	1903
Gillingham	BR(SR)	1957	BR(SR)16	lever frame	30	1957
Gillingham	SE&CR	1913	SEC	lever frame	44	1913
Girvan	G&SWR	1893E	GSW3	lever frame	30	1973
Glasgow Central	BR(ScR)	1961	BR(ScR)PB	panel		1973
Glazebrook East Junction	BR(LMR)	1961	BR(LMR)15	lever frame	80	1961
Glenwhilly	G&SWR	1905	GSW7	lever frame	20	1905
Gloucester	BR(WR)	1968	BR(WR)PB	panel		1968
Gobowen North	GWR	1884	McK&H3	lever frame	16	1912
Godnow Bridge (G)	MS&LR	1886	RSCo	panel		1981
Goodmayes	LNER	1949	LNER15	panels		1949 & 72
Goole	NER	1909	NE S4	panel		1975
Goole Bridge	NER	1869	NE n/s	lever frame & panel	5	1933
Goonbarrow Junction	GWR	1909	GW7d	lever frame	25	1924
Gosberton	GER	1882	GE2	lever frame	30	1882
Gospel Oak	BR(LMR)	1985	BR(LMR) n/s	panel		1985
Goxhill	GCR	1910	GC n/s	lever frame	36	1910
Grain Crossing (G)	SER	1882	Stevens	lever frame	9	nk
Grange Junction	BR(LMR)	1966	BR(LMR)15	lever frame	75	1966
Grange-over-Sands	BR(LMR)	1956	BR(LMR)15	lever frame	25	1956
Grangemouth Junction	NBR	u1882	NB4	lever frame	38	1899
Grangetown	LNER	1954	LNER15	panel		1984
Great Coates Sidings No1	GCR	1909	MS&L3 s/h	lever frame	23	1909
Great Rocks Junction	MR	1923	Mid4d	lever frame	34	1923
Greatham	NER	1889	NE N1	lever frame	21	1941
Greaves Siding (NBP)	GWR	1918	GW7d	lever frame	28	1918
Greenbank	BR(LMR)	1975	BR(LMR)15	panel		1980
Greenfield Junction	LNWR	1888	LNW4	lever frame	12	1888
Greenfoot	CR	nk	Cal S4	lever frame	20	1910
Greenford East Station	GWR	1904E	GW27c	lever frame	76	1956
Greenhill Upper Junction	BR(ScR)	1990	BR(ScR) RR	panel		1990
Greenloaning	CR	1891	Cal N2	lever frame	32	1891
Greetland	LMSR	1942	LMS13	lever frame	55	1942
Gresty Lane No1	LNWR	1899	LNW4	panel		1978
Grindleford	LMSR	1934	LMS11c	lever frame	25	1934
Gristhorpe (G)	NER	1873	NE S1b	lever frame	14	1910
Grove Road (G)	GNR	1880	GN1	panel		1976
Guide Bridge	GCR	1906	GC5	panel		1984

Signalbox Name	Company	Date	Design	Mechanical or Panel	No of Levers	Date of Frame or Panel
Guildford	BR(SR)	1966	BR(SR)19PB	panel		1966
Hackney Downs	BR(ER)	1960	BR(ER)18PB	panel		1960
Hademore Crossing	LNWR	1899	LNW4	lever frame	15	1899
Halifax	L&YR	1884	RSCo	panel		1970
Hall Dene	NER	1905	NE N3	lever frame	21	1942
Halton Junction	LNWR	1897	LNW4	lever frame	24	1897
Hammerton	BR(ER)	1980s	3-sided cover	lever frame	10	1914
Hampden Park	LB&SCR	1888E	LBSC2b	lever frame	24	1930
Hamworthy	L&SWR	1893	LSW3b	lever frame	59	1893
Harlescott Crossing	LNWR	1882E	LNW4	lever frame	38	1882
Harling Road	GER	1883	GE4/McK&H	lever frame	25	1883
Harlow Mill	BR(ER)	1960	BR(ER)18PB	panel		1960
Harringay Park Junction	BR(ER)	1959	BR(ER) n/s	lever frame	25	1959
Harringworth (OOU)	LMSR	1928	Mid4e	lever frame	25	1928
Harrogate	LNER	1947	LNER15	lever frame	45	1947
Hartford Junction	LMS	1925	LNW5	lever frame	54	1925
Hartlebury	GWR	1876	McK&H2	panel		1982
Haslemere	L&SWR	1895	LSW4	lever frame	47	1895
Hastings	SR	1930	SR12	lever frame	84	1930
Havant	LB&SCR	1876E	S&F5	lever frame	64	1938
Hawkesbury Lane	LNWR	1896	LNW4	lever frame	26	1896
Hawkesbury Station Junction	SR	1934	SR12	lever frame	80	1934
Haydon Bridge	NER	1877	NE N1	lever frame	31	1964
Hazel Grove	LNWR	1877	LNW4	panel		1986
Healey Mills	BR(ER)	1963	BR(ER)PB	panel		1963
Heath Junction	BR(WR)	1984	Portakabin	panel		1984
Heaton Norris Junction	BR(LMR)	1955	BR(LMR)14	lever frame	60	1955
Hebden Bridge	L&YR	1891	L&Y	lever frame	38	1891
Heckington	GNR	1876	GN1	lever frame	18	1925
Hednesford No1	LNWR	1877	LNW4	lever frame	38	1877
Heighington	NER	1872	NE C1	lever frame	11	1906
Hellifield South Junction	MR	1911	Mid4c	lever frame	61	1911
Helpston (G)	GNR	1898	GN1	panel		1976
Helsby Junction	LNWR	1900	LNW4	lever frame	45	1900
Hemingbrough	NER	1873	NE S1a	lever frame	21	1905
Henley-in-Arden	GWR	1907	GW7d	lever frame	57	1907
Hensall Station	L&YR	1875	Yardley 1	lever frame & panel	30	1964
Henwick	GWR	1875E	McK&H1	lever frame	25	1897
Henwick Hall (G)	NER	1912	NE S1a	panel		1973
Hereford	LNW&GWJt	1884	LNW&GWJt 2	lever frame & panel	60	1938 & 84
Hertford East	GER	1888	GE7/McK&H	lever frame	45	1888
Hessle Road	BR(ER)	1962	BR(NER)PB	panel		1962
Hest Bank LCF (G)	BR(LMR)	1958	BR(LMR)15	panel		1982
Hexham	NER	u1918	NE N5 o/h	lever frame	60	1918
Hickleton Main Colliery	LMSR	1933	LMS11b	lever frame	50	1933
High Street [Lincoln]	GNR	1874	GN1	lever frame	36	1892
Highams Park (G)	LNER	u1927	LNER11a	lever frame	5	u1927
Hilton Junction	CR	1873	Cal N1	lever frame	20	nk
Hinkley	LNWR	1894	LNW4	lever frame	20	1894
Hither Green (RR)	BR(SR)	1962	BR(SR)18PB			
Holme (G)	BR(ER)	1975	BR(ER)20	panel		1975
Holmes Chapel Frame (NBP)	BR(LMR)	1959	BR(LMR) Hut	lever frame	10	1959
Holmwood	LB&SCR	1877	S&F5	lever frame	18	1877
Holton-le-Moor	MS&LR	1890	MS&L3	panel		1989
Holyhead GF (NBP)	BR(LMR)	1968	BR(LMR)15	lever frame	15	1968

Signalbox Name	Company	Date	Design	Mechanical or Panel	No of Levers	Date of Frame or Panel
Holyhead Station	LMSR	1937	LMS11e	lever frame	100	1937
Holywell Junction	LNWR	1902	LNW4	lever frame	54	1902
Holywood	G&SWR	nk	GSW7	lever frame	23	nk
Honiton	BR(SR)	1957	BR(SR)16	lever frame	24	1957
Hooton	BR(LMR)	1985	Portakabin	panel		1985
Horbury Junction	LMSR	1927	LNW5	lever frame	65	1927
Horrocksford Junction	L&YR	1873	S&F6	lever frame	8	1928
Horsforth	NER	1883	NE S1b	lever frame	15	1916
Horsham	SR	1938	SR13	lever frame	90	1938
Howden	NER	1873	NE S1a	lever frame	15	1905
Howe & Co's Siding	MR	1916	Mid4a	lever frame	30	1947
Howsham (G)	NER	1873	NE S1b	lever frame	9	1891
Hubberts Bridge	BR(ER)	1961	BR(ER) n/s	lever frame	25	1961
Huddersfield	BR(NER)	1958	BR(NER)PB	panel		1993
Hull Paragon	LNER	1938	LNER13PB	panel		1984
Hull River Bridge	NER	1885	S&F	lever frame & panel	6	1885 & 1964
Huncoat Station (G)	L&YR	1902	L&Y	lever frame	8	1902
Hunmanby	NER	1875E	NE S1a	lever frame	16	1908
Huntly	GNoSR	1890	GNoS2	lever frame	25	1970
Hunts Cross	BR(LMR)	1982	BR(LMR)PR	panel		1982
Hurlford	LMSR	1920s	LMS12	lever frame	20	1976
Huyton	LNWR	1899	LNW4	lever frame	36	1899
Ilford Carriage Shed	LNER	1949	LNER15	lever frame & panel	24	1949
Ilford Station	LNER	1949	LNER15	lever frame & panel	15	1949
Immingham East Junction	GCR	1912	GC5	power frame	60	1912
Immingham Reception Sidings	GCR	1912	GC5	power frame	91	1912
Immingham West Junction	GCR	1912	GC5	panel		1975
Ingatestone	GER	1905	GE7	panel		1996
Insch	GNoSR	1886	GNoS2	lever frame	20	1969
Inverkeilor	NBR	1881	NB1	lever frame	22	1881
Inverness	BR(ScR)	1987	BR(ScR)PB	panel		1987
Inverurie	GNoSR	1902	GNoS3	lever frame	30	1970
Jumble Lane	GCR	nk	GC n/s	lever frame	35	nk
Keadby Canal Junction (NBP)	LNER	1926	LNER11a	power frame	36	1926
Keith Junction	GNoSR	1905	GNoS3	lever frame	40	1969
Kennethmont	GNoSR	1888	RSCo Hipped	lever frame	20	1969
Kennett	GER	1880	GE2	lever frame	20	1880
Ketton	MR	1900	Mid2b	lever frame	20	1900
Kew East Junction	NLR	1900	NL3b	lever frame	50	1900
Kidderminster Junction	BR(WR)	1953	BR(WR)16	lever frame	66	1953
Kidsgrove Central	BR(LMR)	1965	BR(LMR)15	lever frame	50	1965
Kidwelly	BR(WR)	1950s	BR(WR)35	panel		1983
Kilkerran	G&SWR	1895	GSW3	lever frame	20	1973
Kilmarnock	BR(ScR)	1976	BR(ScR)PB	panel		1976
Kingmoor (RR)	BR(LMR)	1963	BR(LMR)PB			
King's Cross	BR(ER)	1971	BR(ER)PB	panel		1970
King's Dyke	GER	1899	GE7/Dutton	lever frame	17	1899
King's Lynn Junction	GER	1881	GE2	lever frame	49	nk
Kingsbury ShuntingFrame (NBP)	BR(LMR)	1969	BR(LMR)15	lever frame	20	1969
Kingswinford Junction South	GWR	1916	GW27c	lever frame	77	1924
Kingussie	HR	nk	McK&H3/HR	lever frame	17	u1922
Kirkby Stephen West	BR(LMR)	1974	BR(LMR)15	lever frame	20	1974

Signalbox Name	Company	Date	Design	Mechanical or Panel	No of Levers	Date of Frame or Panel
Kirkconnel	G&SWR	1911	GSW7	lever frame	24	1911
Kirkham Abbey	NER	1873	NE S1a	lever frame	16	1926
Kirkham North Junction	L&YR	1903	L&Y	lever frame	57	1903
Kirton Lime Sidings	MS&LR	1886	RSCo	lever frame	15	1886
Kiveton Park Station	MS&LR	nk	GC5	panel		1980
Knaresborough	NER	1873	NE n/s	lever frame	12	1950
Knottingley	BR(NER)	1967	BR(NER)17	panel		1967
Knutsford East (OOU)	CLC	1886	Stevens n/s	lever frame	20	1886
Lakenheath	GER	1885	GE4/S&F	lever frame	25	1885
Lancing	BR(SR)	1963	BR(SR)16	panel		1988
Langham Junction	MR	1890	Mid2a	lever frame	20	1890
Langworth	MS&LR	1890	MS&L3	panel		1990
Larbert Junction	CR	1871	Cal n/s	lever frame	40	1915
Larbert North	CR	1892	Cal N2	lever frame	59	nk
Laurencekirk	CR	1910	Cal N2	lever frame	40	1910
Leamington Spa	BR(LMR)	1985	BR(LMR)PB	panel		1985
Ledbury	GWR	1885	McK&H3	lever frame	42	nk
Leeds	BR(LMR)	1967		panel		1967
Leicester	BR(LMR)	1986	BR(LMR)PB	panel & VDUs		1986
Leigh	NSR	nk	NS2	lever frame	25	nk
Leominster	LNW&GWJt	1875	LNW&GWJt 1	lever frame	30	1941
Leuchars	NBR	1920	NB8	lever frame	38	1920
Lewes	LB&SCR	1888	S&F5	panel		1976
Lichfield Trent Valley Junction	LNWR	1897	LNW4	lever frame	45	1897
Lichfield Trent Valley No 1	LNWR	1911	LNW5	lever frame	80	1911
Lightmoor Junction	BR(WR)	1951	BR(WR)15	lever frame	31	1951
Lime Kiln Sidings	GWR	1887	GW3	lever frame	29	1918
Lincoln Street	MR	1916	Mid4a	lever frame	12	1916
Liskeard	GWR	1915	GW27c	lever frame	36	1915
Little Mill Junction	GWR	1883E	McK&H3	lever frame & panel	17	1938 & 79
Littlehampton	LB&SCR	1886	LBSC2a	lever frame	44	1901
Littlehaven (G)	SR	1938	SR SB&BO	lever frame	8	1938
Littleport	GER	1882	GE2	lever frame	25	1882
Littleworth	GNR	1875	GN1	lever frame	30	1875
Litton's Mill Crossing	LNWR	1890	LNW4	lever frame	18	1922
Liverpool Lime Street	LMSR	1948	LMS13	power frame	95	1948
Liverpool Street IECC	BR(LMR)	1989	BRPB	VDUs etc		1989
Llandaff Loop Junction	TVR	1900	TVR	lever frame	40	1966
Llandarcy (NBP)	GWR	1920	GW7d	lever frame	20	1920
Llanelli West (G)	GWR	1877E	GW2	panel	nk	
Llandudno	LNWR	1891	LNW4	lever frame	34	1891
Llandudno Junction	BR(LMR)	1985	BR(LMR)15	panel		1985
Llanfair PG (G)	LNWR	1871	LNW/C&H	lever frame	4	1883
Llanrwst & Trefriw	LNWR	1880	LNW4	lever frame	20	1954
Lock Lane Crossing SF (G)	BR(LMR)	1955	BR(LMR)15	lever frame	10	1955
London Bridge	BR(SR)	1975	BR(SR)PB	panel		1975
Long Lane	NER	1873	NE S1b	lever frame	17	1905
Longannet	BR(ScR)	1969	BR(ScR) n/s	lever frame	30	1969
Longbeck	LNER	1932	LNER12	panel		1970
Longbridge East (NBP)	MR	1916	Mid4a	lever frame	36	1917
Longforgan	LMSR	1929	LMS12	lever frame	20	1929
Longport Junction	LMSR	1939	LMS11c	lever frame	50	1970
Lostwithiel	GWR	1893	GW5	lever frame	63	1923
Low Gates	BR(NER)	1956	BR(NER)16b	panel		1992
Low House Crossing	MR	1900	Mid2b	lever frame	12	1900

Signalbox Name	Company	Date	Design	Mechanical or Panel	No of Levers	Date of Frame or Panel
Low Row	NER	1874	NE N1	lever frame	29	1957
Lowdham	MR	1896	Mid2b	lever frame	16	1896
Lowestoft	GER	1885	GE6	lever frame	61	1905
Lugton	LMSR	1929	LMS12	lever frame	35	u1938
Lydney Crossing GF (G)	GWR	1918	GW27c	panel		1969
Macclesfield	BR(LMR)	1965	BR(LMR)15	lever frame	55	1965
Machynlleth	BR(WR)	1960	BR(WR)37	lever frame & RETB	50	1965 & 88
Madeley	LMSR	1930	LMS11b	lever frame	40	1930
Madeley Junction	BR(LMR)	1969	BR(LMR)15	lever frame	40	1969
Maesmawr	GWR	1930	GW28	lever frame	65	1930
Magdalen Road Junction	LNER	1927	GC5 s/h	panel		1992
Maidstone East	BR(SR)	1962	BR(SR)18	power frame & panels	47	1962 & 83 & 84
Maidstone West	SE&CR	1899	EOD	lever frame	115	1899
Mallaig (NBP)	NBR	1901	RSCo/WHE	lever frame	4	1901
Maltby Colliery South	GCR	1912	GC5	lever frame	36	1912
Malton	NER	1873	NE S1a	panel		1966
Malvern Wells	GWR	1919	GW7d	lever frame	40	1919
Manchester Piccadilly	BR(LMR)	1988		panel		1988
Manchester Victoria East Junction	BR(LMR)	1962	BR(LMR)PB	panel		1962
Manea	GER	1883	GE3/McK&H	lever frame	26	1883
Mantle Lane	MR	1910	Mid4c	lever frame	28	1910
Manton Junction	MR	1913	Mid4c	panel		1988
March East Junction	GER	1885	GE5/S&F	lever frame	58	1897
March South Junction	LNER	1927	LNER11a	lever frame	50	1927
Marcheys House	NER	1895	NE N2	lever frame	15	1960
Margate	SR	1926	SEC	lever frame	80	1926
Marks Tey	GER	1890sE	GE7	lever frame	60	1941
Marsh Brook	LNW&GWJt	1872	LNW&GWJt 1	lever frame	18	nk
Marsh Junction	GCR	1908	GC5	lever frame	44	1908
Marston Moor (G)	NER	1910	NE S5	lever frame	16	1910
Marylebone IECC	BR(LMR)	1990		VDUs etc		1990
Maryport	LMSR	1933	LMS11b	lever frame & panel	50	1933 & 79
Mauchline No1	G&SWR	1877	GSW1	lever frame	35	1978
Meaford Crossing	NSR	1880	NS1	lever frame	16	1880
Medge Hall (G)	MS&LR	1886	RSCo	lever frame	7	1886
Melton Lane	NER	1921	NE S4	lever frame & panel	26	1921 & 80
Melton Station	LMSR	1942	LMS11c	lever frame	45	1942
Methley Junction	MR	1891	Mid2a	lever frame	26	1891
Mickle Trafford	BR(LMR)	1969	BR(LMR)15	lever frame	35	1969
Middlesbrough	NER	1877	NE C1	panel		1978
Midge Hall	BR(LMR)	1972	BR(LMR)15	lever frame	20	1972
Mile End (RR)	LNER	1949	LNER15PB			
Miles Platting Junction	L&YR	1890	RSCo	lever frame	92	1890
Milford	BR(NER)	1957	BR(NER)17	panel		1982
Mill Green	GER	1882	GE2	lever frame	21	1931
Mill Lane Junction	L&YR	1884	RSCo	panel		1973
Millbrook Dock Gates (G)	SR	u1936	Dock Gates House	panel		nk
Millbrook Station	LNWR	u1870	LNW Hut	lever frame	10	1990
Millerhill	BR(ScR)	1988	BR(ScR)PB	panel		1988
Millom	FR	1917	Furness	lever frame	28	u1891
Milner Royd Junction	L&YR	1878	Yardley 2	lever frame	20	1903
Milton (G)	NER	1893	NE N2	lever frame	10	1893
Minster	SR	1929	SR12	lever frame	70	1929
Mobberley	CLC	1886	CLC1b	panel		1991
Moira West Junction	MR	1896	Mid2b	panel		1986

Signalbox Name	Company	Date	Design	Mechanical or Panel	No of Levers	Date of Frame or Panel
Mold Junction No1	LNWR	1902	LNW4	lever frame	30	1902
Monks Siding	LNWR	1875	LNW3	lever frame	20	1875
Monkwearmouth	NER	u1876	NE N1	lever frame	30	1939
Montrose North	NBR	1881	NB1	lever frame	51	1953
Montrose South	NBR	1881	NB1	lever frame	42	nk
Moorthorpe	MR	1908	Mid4c	lever frame	36	1908
Moreton-in-Marsh	GWR	1883	GW4b	lever frame	40	1911
Moreton-on-Lugg	GWR	1943	GW12a	lever frame	44	1943
Morpeth	BR(ER)	1978	BR(ER)20	panel		1991
Morton Crossing GF (G, OOU)	LMSR	nk	MR Hut	lever frame	10	1929
Moss	NER	1873	NE S1a	lever frame	11	1940
Mostyn	LNWR	1902	LNW4	lever frame	40	1902
Motherwell	BR(ScR)	1972	BR(ScR)PB	panel		1972 & 94
Mouldsworth Junction	CLC	1894	CLC1a	lever frame	34	1894
Mountfield GF (NBP)	BR(SR)	nk	BR(SR) Hut	lever frame	11	nk
Mow Cop	BR(LMR)	nk	NS2	panel		1981
Nairn East	HR	1891	McK&H3/HR	lever frame	13	1891
Nairn West	HR	1891	McK&H3/HR	lever frame	19	nk
Nantwich	BR(LMR)	1948	LMS11c s/h	lever frame	30	1948
Narborough	LNWR	1875	LNW3	panel		1986
Neasden Junction	MR	1899	Mid2b	lever frame	24	1899
Neath & Brecon Junction	GWR	1892	GW5	lever frame	14	1957
Netherfield Junction	BR(ER)	1960	BR(ER) n/s	lever frame	40	1960
New Cumnock	G&SWR	1909	GSW7	lever frame	40	1909
New Hythe	SR	1939	SR13	lever frame	20	1939
New Mills Junction	LMSR	1924	Mid4d	lever frame	30	1924
New Mills South Junction	MR	1903	Mid3b	lever frame	55	nk
Newark	MR	1912	Mid4a	lever frame	16	1912
Newhaven Harbour	LB&SCR	1886	S&F5	lever frame	42	1886
Newhaven Town	LB&SCR	1879	S&F5	lever frame	40	1953
Newland East	GWR	1900	GW7a	lever frame	33	nk
Newport	BR(WR)	1962	BR(WR)PB	panels		1962 & 68
Newsham South	NER	nk	NE N1	lever frame	20	1945
Newtonhill	CR	1876	Cal N1	lever frame	30	1907
Norbury Crossing (G)	BR(LMR)	1974	BR(LMR)15	gf	5	1974
North Seaton (G)	NER	u1872	NE n/s	lever frame	21	1950
North Side StaithesGF (NBP)	SR	1926	Hut	lever frame	6	1926
North Walsham	GER	1896	GE7	lever frame	31	u1896
Northampton Bridge Street Level Crossing	LNWR	1907	LNW5	lever frame	15	1907
Northenden Junction	CLC	nk	Stevens n/s	lever frame	25	nk
Northfleet	BR(SR)	1970	BR(SR) n/s	panel		1970
Northorpe	MS&LR	1886	RSCo	lever frame	17	1886
Norton	BR(LMR)	1972	BR(LMR)15	lever frame	10	1972
Norton (G)	BR(ER)	1980	BR(ER)20	panel		1980
Norton Bridge	BR(LMR)	1961	BR(LMR)PB	panel		1961
Norton East	NER	1870	NE n/s	lever frame	25	1959
Norton Junction	GWR	1908	GW7d	lever frame	19	1908
Norton South	NER	1870	NE n/s	lever frame	20	1955
Norton West	NER	u1921	NE S4	lever frame	41	1921
Norton-on-Tees	NER	1897	NEC2a	lever frame	26	1957
Nuneaton	BR(LMR)	1963	BR(LMR)PB	panel		1990
Nunthorpe	NER	1903	NE C2b	lever frame	16	1966
Oakenshaw	LMSR	1928	Mid4e	panel		1965
Oakham Level Crossing	MR	1899	Mid2b	lever frame	17	1899

Signalbox Name	Company	Date	Design	Mechanical or Panel	No of Levers	Date of Frame or Panel
Oddingley (G)	MR	1908	Mid3a	none		
Offord (G)	BR(ER)	1976	BR(ER)20	panel		1976
Old Oak Common (RR)	BR(WR)	1962	BR(WR)PB			
Oldham Mumps	BR(LMR)	1967	BR(LMR)15 s/h	lever frame	50	1967
Olive Mount Junction	LNWR	1883	LNW4	lever frame	36	1883
Ollerton Colliery	LNER	1926	GC5	lever frame & panel	30	1926 & 84
Onibury	BR(WR)	1977	BR(WR)37	panel		1977
Oulton Broad North Junction	GER	1901E	GE7	lever frame	36	1901
Oulton Broad Swing Bridge (NBP)	GER	1907	GE7	lever frame	10	1907
Oxford	BR(WR)	1973	BR(WR)PB	panel		1973
Oxley	BR(LMR)	1969	BR(LMR)15	lever frame	60	1969
Oxmardyke (G)	NER	1901	NE S1a	lever frame	16	1956
Oxmarsh Crossing	BR(ER)	1959	BR(ER)16a	lever frame	29	1885
Oxted	BR(SR)	1987	BR(SR)PB	panel		1987
Paddock Wood (E)	BR(SR)	1962	BR(SR)PR	panel		1962
Paignton	BR(WR)	1989		panel		1989
Paisley	BR(ScR)	1985	BR(ScR)PB	panel		1985
Paisley (RR)	BR(ScR)	1966	BR(ScR)PB			
Pantyffynnon South	GWR	1892	GW5	lever frame	49	1892
Par	GWR	1879E	GW2	lever frame & panel	57	1913 & 86
Parbold	L&YR	1877	S&F9	lever frame		1983
Park Junction	GWR	1885E	McK&H3	lever frame	100	1920
Park South	FR	1883	Furness 3	lever frame	24	1962
Parkeston	BR(ER)	u1987	BR(ER)PB	panel		u1987
Parton	LNWR	1879	LNW4	lever frame	28	1879
Pasture Street	BR(ER)	1961	BR(ER)19	panel		1985
Peak Forest South	LMSR	1925	Mid4d	lever frame	50	1974
Peckfield	NER	u1873	NE S1a	lever frame	20	1907
Pelham Street Junction	GNR	u1874	GN1	lever frame	100	1918
Pembrey	GWR	1907	GW7	lever frame	83	1953
Pencoed Crossing GF (G)	GWR	1905	GW27c	panel		nk
Penistone	MS&LR	1888	MS&L2	lever frame	29	1953
Penmaenmawr	BR(LMR)	1952	BR(LMR)14	lever frame	25	1952
Penyffordd	BR(LMR)	1972	BR(LMR)15	lever frame	25	1972
Penzance	GWR	1938	GW12b	lever frame	75	1938
Perth	BR(ScR)	1962	BR(ScR)PB	panel		1962
Peterborough	BR(ER)	1972	BR(ER)PB	panel		1972
Petersfield GF (NBP)	SR	nk	SR Hut	lever frame	15	nk
Petersfield	L&SWR	1880s	LSW3a	lever frame & panel	10	1880s & 1974
Pevensey	LB&SCR	1876	S&F5	lever frame	14	1876
Philips Park No1	L&YR	1889	RSCo	lever frame	64	1889
Philips Park No2	L&YR	1889	RSCo	lever frame	30	1889
Picton	NER	1873	NE S1a	lever frame	26	1905
Pinxton	MR	1897	Mid2b	lever frame	28	1897
Pitlochry	HR	1911	Highland	lever frame	24	u1911
Plean Junction	CR	1870s	Cal N1	lever frame	20	1922
Plumley West	CLC	1908	CLC2	lever frame	26	1908
Plumpton (G)	LB&SCR	1891	LBSC2b	lever frame	21	1891
Plumpton Junction	FR	1898	Furness 4	lever frame	49	1898
Plymouth	BR(WR)	1960	BR(WR)PB	panel		1960
Polegate Crossing	LB&SCR	1883	S&F5	lever frame	20	1883
Polmaise	CR	1905	Cal N3	lever frame	70	1948
Polmont	BR(ScR)	1979	BR(ScR)PR	panel		1979
Pontrilas	GWR	1880	McK&H3	lever frame	42	1910

Signalbox Name	Company	Date	Design	Mechanical or Panel	No of Levers	Date of Frame or Panel
Pontypridd Junction	TVR	1902	Taff Vale	lever frame	70	1902
Poole	L&SWR	1897E	LSW4	lever frame	51	u1897
Poppleton	NER	1870sE	NE S1	lever frame	11	1941
Port Talbot	BR(WR)	1963	BR(WR)PB	panel		1963
Porth	BR(WR)	1981	BR(WR) n/s	lever frame	16	1981
Portsmouth	BR(SR)	1968	BR(SR)19PB	panel		1968
Poulton No3	L&YR	1896	L&Y	lever frame	74	1896
Prees	LNWR	1881	LNW4	lever frame	25	1881
Prescot	BR(LMR)	1953	LNW5	lever frame	30	1953
Prestatyn	LNWR	1897	LNW4	lever frame	45	1897
Preston	BR(LMR)	1972	BR(LMR)PB	panel		1972
Prudhoe	NER	1872E	NE N1	lever frame	45	1944
Pulborough	LB&SCR	1878	S&F5	lever frame	30	1952
Puxton & Worle (G)	GWR	1916	GW7d	panel		1972
Pwllheli West Frame (NBP)	GWR	1907	Dutton2 (McK&H)	lever frame	4	1907
Pyewipe Road	BR(ER)	1958	BR(ER)16a	lever frame	20	1958
Quay Crossing, (Bridlington)	NER	1911	NE S4	lever frame	42	1911
Radyr Junction	BR(WR)	1961	BR(WR)37 s/h	lever frame	107	1961
Radyr Quarry Junction	TVR	1899	Taff Vale	lever frame	61	1946
Rainford Junction	LMS	1933	LMS11c	lever frame	10	nk
Rainham	BR(SR)	1959	BR(SR)17PB	panel		1959
Ramsgate	SR	1926	SR11a	lever frame	96	1926
Ranelagh Road Crossing (G)	LNER	1927	LNER n/s	lever frame	10	1927
Ranskill (G)	GNR	1875	GN1	panel		1975
Rauceby	GNR	1880	GN1	lever frame & panel	5	1975
Reading	BR(WR)	1965	BR(WR)PB	panels		1965 & 77
Rectory Junction	GNR	1889	GN3	lever frame	64	1889
Redcar	LNER	1937	LNER13	panel		1970
Reedham Junction	GER	1904	GE7	lever frame	60	1904
Reedham Swing Bridge	GER	1904	GE7	lever frame	12	1904
Reigate	SR	1929	SR11b	lever frame	24	1929
Retford Thrumpton	MS&LR	1889	MS&L3	panel		1965
Rhyl [No1]	LNWR	1900	LNW4	lever frame	90	1900
Ribble Yard GF (NBP)	BR(LMR)	nk	BR(LMR)15	lever frame	20	nk
Richmond	SR	1940	SR13	panel		1980
Rigton	NER	1873u	NE S1a	lever frame	6	1939
Robertsbridge	SER	1894	S&F12a	lever frame	23	1894
Rochdale	L&YR	1889	RSCo	lever frame	30	nk
Rochester	BR(SR)	1959	BR(SR)17 PB	panel		1959
Rock Ferry	BR(LMR)	1957	BR(LMR)15	panel		1994
Romford	LNER	1931	LNER11c	lever frame & panel	40	1931 & 49
Romiley Junction	MR	1899	Mid2b	panel		1980
Roskear Junction	GWR	1895	GW5	panel		nk
Rosyth Dockyard	NBR	1917	NB7	lever frame	45	u1917
Roxton Sidings	MS&LR	1884	MS&L2	lever frame	18	1884
Roydon	GER	1876E	GE1/S&F	lever frame	27	1959
Royston Junction	MR	1901	Mid3b	lever frame	80	1958
Rufford	BR(LMR)	1988	Portakabin	panel		1988
Rugby	BR(LMR)	1964	BR(LMR)PB	panel		1964
Runcorn	LMS	1944	LMS13	lever frame	45	1944
Ryde St Johns Road	SR	1928	EOD	lever frame & panel	40	1928 & 89
Rye	SER	1894	S&F12a	lever frame	30	1894
Ryhope Grange Junction	NER	1905	NE N3	lever frame	40	1950
Salisbury	BR(WR)	1981		panel (in parcels office)		1981
Salop Goods Junction	LNWR	1901	LNW4	lever frame	65	1936
Saltley	BR(LMR)	1969	BR(LMR)PB	panel		1969

Signalbox Name	Company	Date	Design	Mechanical or Panel	No of Levers	Date of Frame or Panel
Saltmarshe	NER	1905	NE S2	lever frame	19	1905
Salwick	L&YR	1889	RSCo	lever frame	35	1889
Sandbach	BR(LMR)	1959	BR(LMR)PB	panel		1959
Sandhills IECC	Merseyrail	1994	industrial unit	VDUs, etc		1994
Sandwich	SR	1938	SR11b	panel		nk
Sandycroft	LNWR	1900	LNW4	lever frame	60	1900
Saxby Junction (OOU)	MR	1892	Mid2a	lever frame	60	1962
Saxilby	LNER	1939	LNER11b	lever frame	30	1939
Saxmundham	GER	1881	GE2	panel & RETB		1985
Scopwick	LNER	1937	LNER11a	lever frame	25	1937
Scropton	NSR	1880s	NS2	lever frame	23	1880s
Scunthorpe	BR(ER)	1973	BR(ER)PB	panel		1973
Scunthorpe Hump (NBP)	BR(ER)	1972	BR(ER) n/s	panel		1972
Seaford	LB&SCR	1895	LBSC2c	lever frame	24	1895
Seaham	NER	1905	NE N3	lever frame	23	1950
Seamer East	NER	1910	NE S4	lever frame	35	1910
Seamer West	NER	1906	NE S4	lever frame	60	1906
Selby	NER	1870sE	NE S1	panel		1973
Selby Swing Bridge (NBP)	NER	1891	NE n/s	gf & 2 panels	2	1970s
Selhurst Depot (NBP)	BR(SR)	(1985)		panel		1985
Sellafield	FR	1918	Furness 4	lever frame	49	1918
Settle Junction	MR	1913	Mid4c	lever frame	31	1960
Seven Sisters Junction	GER	1905E	GE7	lever frame	48	1905
Seymour Junction	BR(ER)	1963	BR(ER)19	lever frame	30	1963
Shaftholme Junction (E)	BR(NER)	1958	BR(NER)PB	panel		1980
Shalford	BR(SR)	1954	BR(SR)16	lever frame	28	1954
Shaw Station	L&YR	u1925	L&Y	lever frame	24	u1925
Sheffield	BR(ER)	1973	BR(ER)PB	panel		1973
Shepherdswell	LC&DR	1878	LCD	lever frame	23	1878
Shildon	NER	1887	NE C2a	lever frame	42	1928
Shippea Hill	GER	1883	GE4/McK&H	lever frame	30	u1883
Shireoaks Station	MS&LR	1874	S&F	panel		1980
Shirebrook Junction	MR	1899E	Mid2b	lever frame	40	1928
Shirebrook Station	MR	1890	Mid2a	lever frame	16	1979
Shireoaks East Junction	GCR	1914	GC5	lever frame	35	1914
Shirley	GWR	1907	GW7d	lever frame	31	1907
Shrewsbury Crewe Bank	LMSR	1943	LMS13	lever frame	45	1943
Shrewsbury Crewe Junction	LNW&GWJt	1903	LNW4	lever frame	120	1903
Shrewsbury Severn Bridge Junction	LNWR	1903	LNW4	lever frame	180	1903
Sibsey	GNR	1888	GN1	panel		1989
Sighthill Junction	NBR	1886	NB1/4	lever frame	95	1930s & 93
Silecroft	FR	1923	Furness 4	lever frame	15	1923
Singleton	L&YR	1879	S&F9	lever frame	16	1922
Sittingbourne	BR(SR)	1959	BR(SR)17PB	panel		1959
Skegness	GNR	1883E	GN1	lever frame	80	1900
Skiers Spring	BR (ER)	1990	Portakabin	panel		1990
Sleaford East	GNR	1882	GN1	lever frame	50	1882
Sleaford North	GN&GE J Rly	1882	GE2	lever frame	18	1882
Sleaford South	BR(ER)	1957	BR(ER)16a	lever frame	25	1957
Sleaford West	GNR	u1880	GN1	lever frame	46	u1880
Sleights Sidings East	MR	1892	Mid2a	panel		1979
Slough	BR(WR)	1963	BR(WR)PB	panel		1963
Slough IECC	BR(WR)	1992		VDUs, etc		1992
Smithy Bridge	L&YR	1907	L&Y	panel		1981
Sneinton Junction (G)	MR	1914	Mid4c	lever frame	10	1914

Signalbox Name	Company	Date	Design	Mechanical or Panel	No of Levers	Date of Frame or Panel
Snodland	SER	u1870s	SE	lever frame	26	u1870s
Snowdown Colliery	BR(SR)	1953	BR(SR) n/s	lever frame	18	1953
Somerleyton Swing Bridge	GER	1904	GE7	lever frame	14	1904
South Tottenham	GER	1894	GE7	panel		1977
Southend East (OOU)	LMS	1932	LMS11b	lever frame & panel	30	1932 & 60
Spalding No1	GNR	1921	GN4b	panel		1984
Speke Junction	LNWR	1907	LNW5	lever frame	86	1907
Spelbrook	GER	1898	GE7	lever frame	24	1898
Spooner Row	GER	1881	GE2	lever frame	15	u1881
St Andrews Junction	GWR	1910	GW27c	panel		1988 & 93
St Ann's Crossing (G,E)	LC&DR	nk	LCD Hut	none		
St Bees	FR	1891	Furness 3	lever frame	24	1891
St Blazey Junction	GWR	1908	GW7d	lever frame	41	1908
St Erth	GWR	1899	GW5	lever frame	69	1929
St Germans	BR(WR)	1973		panel		1973
St Helens Station	LNWR	1891	LNW4	lever frame	24	1891
St James Deeping	GNR	1876	GN1	lever frame	32	1941
St Leonards West Marina	LB&SCR	1891	S&F5	lever frame	40	1891
St Margarets	GER	1887	GE7/McK&H	lever frame	55	1887
St Nicholas Deeping	GNR	1876	GN1	lever frame		
St Mary's Crossing (G)	GWR	1870s	GW2	none		
Stafford No4	BR(LMR)	1960	BR(LMR)15	lever frame	105	1960
Stafford No5	BR(LMR)	1952	BR(LMR)14	lever frame	150	1952
Stallingborough	MS&LR	1884	MS&L2	lever frame	20	1884
Stalybridge	MS&LR	1886	Stevens/MS&L	lever frame	70	1942
Stanley Junction	BR(ScR)	1961	BR(ScR) n/s	lever frame	45	1961
Stanlow & Thornton	LMSR	1941	LMS11c	lever frame	50	1941
Stanton Gate (NBP)	BR(LMR)	1969	BR(LMR)15	lever frame	50	1969
Stapleford & Sandiacre (NBP)	BR(LMR)	1949	BR(LMR)14	lever frame	115	1949
Starbeck South	NER	nk	NE S1a	lever frame	26	1915
Staythorpe Crossing	BR(LMR)	1950E	LMS11c	lever frame	35	1959
Stechford Shunting Frame (NBP)	LNWR	nk	LNW5	lever frame	23	nk
Stirling Middle	CR	1901	Cal N2	lever frame	96	1901
Stirling North	CR	1900	Cal N2	lever frame	48	1950
Stockport No1	LNWR	1884	LNW4	lever frame	96	1884
Stockport No2	LNWR	1890	LNW4	lever frame	90	1890
Stoke	BR(LMR)	1966	BR(LMR)PB	panel		1966
Stone Crossing (G)	SE&CR	u1904	SE	lever frame	5	1971
Stonea	BR(ER)	1984	Portakabin	panel		1984
Stonehaven	CR	1901	Cal N2	lever frame	40	1901
Stourbridge Junction	GWR	1901	GW7b	lever frame	60	1990
Stourton	BR(WR)	1981	Portakabin	panel		1981
Stow Park	GNR	1877	GN1	lever frame	32	1877
Stow (G)	GER	1881	GE2	lever frame	17	1881
Stowmarket (G)	GER	1882	GE3	panel		1985
Stranraer Harbour	GSWR	1897	GSW3	lever frame	56	u1897
Stranton	NER	1911	NE N4	lever frame	30	1950
Stratford	LNER	1949	LNER15	panels		1967 & 84
Stratford-on-Avon	GWR	1933	GW27c	lever frame	55	1933
Strensall	NER	1901	NE S2	panel		1988
Sturry (G)	SER	1893	S&F12a	lever frame	19	1893
Sudbury	NSR	1885	NS1	lever frame	26	1885
Sudforth Lane	BR(NER)	1959	BR(NER)17	panel		1968
Sunderland	BR(NER)	1965	BR(NER)PB	panel		1965

Signalbox Name	Company	Date	Design	Mechanical or Panel	No of Levers	Date of Frame or Panel
Surbiton	BR(SR)	1970	BR(SR)19PB	panel		1970
Sutton Bridge Junction	LNW&GWJt	1913	GW7	lever frame	61	1913
Swinderby	MR	1901	Mid3a	lever frame	16	1901
Swindon	BR(WR)	1968	BR(WR)PB	panel		1968
Swindon B	RailTrack	1993		panel		1993
Swing Bridge East	NBR	1899	NB n/s	lever frame	15	1983
Talacre	LNWR	1903	LNW4	lever frame	24	1903
Tallington (G)	BR(ER)	1975	BR(ER)20	panel		1975
Tamworth Low Level	LNWR	1910	LNW5	lever frame	35	1910
Tay Bridge South	NBR	1887	NB2a	lever frame	27	1887
Templecombe	SR	1938	SR13	lever frame	16	1938
Thames Haven SH	BR(ER)	1973	BR(ER) Hut	panels		1973, 83, 83
Thetford	GER	1883	GE4/McK&H	lever frame	33	u1883
Thoresby Colliery	LNER	1926	GC5	lever frame	30	1926
Thornhill	LMSR	1943	LMS13	lever frame	30	1943
Thorpe Culvert	GNR	1888	GN1	lever frame	22	1899
Thorpe Gates (G)	NER	1873E	NE S1a	panel		1973
Thorpe-le-Soken	GER	1882E	GE2	panel		1989
Thorpes Bridge Junction	BR(LMR)	1987	Portakabins	panel		1987
Three Bridges	BR(SR)	1983	BR(SR)PB	panel		1983
Three Horse Shoes	GER	1901	GE7	lever frame	30	1901
Three Spires Junction OOU	LNWR	1914	LNW5	panel		c1988
Tinsley Yard	BR(ER)	1965	BR(ER)18PB	panel		1965
Tonbridge	BR(SR)	1962	BR(SR)18PB	panel		1962
Tondu	GWR	1884	GW3	lever frame	65	1963
Totley Tunnel East	MR	1893	Mid2b	lever frame	12	1893
Towneley LCF (G)	L&YR	1878	S&F9	panel		1979
Tram Inn	GWR	1894	GW5	lever frame	23	1978
Trent	BR(LMR)	1969	BR(LMR)PB	panel		1969
Trimley	BR(ER)	1988	Portakabin	panel		1988
Tring Carriage Sidings Frame (NBP)	BR(LMR)	1964	BR(LMR)15	lever frame	10	1964
Truro	GWR	1899	GW7a	lever frame	54	1971
Tunnel Junction	GWR	1905	GW7	lever frame	58	1960
Tutbury Crossing	NSR	1872	McK&H1	lever frame	9	1897
Tweedmouth	BR(NER)	1961	BR(NER)PB	panel		1991
Ty Croes (G)	LNWR	1872	LNW/C&H	lever frame	6	1901
Tyneside IECC	BR(ER)	1991	BR(ER)PB	VDUs etc		1991
Tyseley No1 (NBP)	BR(WR)	1949	GW14	lever frame	30	1949
Uffington & Barnack	MR	1909	Mid4a	lever frame	16	1909
Ulceby Junction	GCR	1910	GC5	lever frame	30	1910
Ulverston	FR	1900	Furness 4	lever frame	22	1900
Upminster IECC	Railtrack	1994		VDUs, etc		1994
Upper Holloway	BR(ER)	1985	Portakabins	panel		1985
Urlay Nook	NER	1896E	NE C2a	lever frame	41	1943
Usan	NBR	1906	NB n/s	lever frame	16	u1906
Uttoxeter	BR(LMR)	1981	BR(LMR)15	lever frame	40	1981
Valley	LNWR	1904	LNW5	lever frame	25	1904
Vauxhall Shunting Frame	BR(LMR)	1957	BR(LMR)15	lever frame	20	1957
Victoria Signalling Centre	BR(SR)	1980	BR(SR)PB	panel		1980 & 92
Vitriol Works	BR(LMR)	1954	BR(LMR)14	lever frame	65	1954
Wainfleet	GNR	1899	GN1	lever frame	25	1899
Wakefield	BR(ER)	1982	Portakabin	panel		1982
Walkden	L&YR	1888	RSCo	lever frame	24	1888
Walnut Tree Junction	TVR	1910s	Taff Vale	lever frame	79	1951

Signalbox Name	Company	Date	Design	Mechanical or Panel	No of Levers	Date of Frame or Panel
Walsall	BR(LMR)	1965	BR(LMR)PB	panel		1965
Wardley	BR(NER)	1954	BR(NER)16b	lever frame	15	1954
Ware	BR(ER)	1960	BR(ER)18	lever frame	20	1960
Wareham	SR	1928	LSW4	lever frame	30	1928
Warnham	LB&SCR	1877	S&F5	lever frame	20	1877
Warrington	BR(LMR)	1972	BR(LMR)PB	panel		1972
Warrington Central	BR(LMR)	1973	BR(LMR)15 s/h	lever frame	55	1973
Washwood Heath Sidings No1 (NBP)	MR	1899	Mid3b	lever frame	80	1924
Wateringbury	SER	1893	S&F12a	lever frame	9	1893
Waterloo (W&C)	L&SWR	1898	LSW n/s	lever frame	16	1898
Waterloo SCC	BR(SR)	1990	BR(SR)PB	panel		1990
Watery Lane Shunting Frame (G)	LMSR	1942	LMS13	lever frame	50	1942
Watford	BR(LMR)	1964	BR(LMR)PB	panel		1964
Weaver Junction	BR(LMR)	1961	BR(LMR) n/s	panel		1961
Weaverthorpe	NER	1873	NE S1a	lever frame	16	1933
Welbeck Colliery Junction	GCR	1915	GC5	lever frame	48	1915
Wellington No2	BR(WR)	1953	BR(WR)15	lever frame	71	1953
Welton (G)	NER	1904	NE S2	lever frame	19	1904
Wem	LNWR	1883	LNW4	lever frame	35	1943
Wennington Junction	MR	1890	Mid2a	lever frame	27	1890
West Burton	BR(ER)	1965	BR(ER)18PB	panel		1965
West Hampstead	BR(LMR)	1979	BR(LMR)PB	panel		1979
West Holmes	GN&GE J Rly	1882	GE2/GN	lever frame	69	1907
West Street Junction (Boston)	GNR	1874	GN1	lever frame	36	1894
Westbury	BR(WR)	1984	BR(WR)PB	panel		1984
Westerfield Junction	GER	1912	GE7	lever frame	48	1912
Western Junction	NLR	1891	NL3a	panel		1987
Whissendine	LMSR	1940	Mid4d s/h	lever frame	20	1940
Whitchurch	LNWR	1897	LNW4	lever frame	55	1897
White Notley (G)	BR(ER)	1977	BR(ER)BO/SB	panel		1977
Whitehouse	NER	1874E	NE C1	lever frame	40	1940
Whitland	BR(WR)	1972	BR(WR)37b s/h	lever frame	39	1972
Whitlingham Junction	GER	1909	GE7	lever frame	34	1909
Whittlesea	GER	1887	GE7	lever frame	26	1887
Whitwell	MR	1893	Mid2b	lever frame	42	1954
Whitwood	NER	1890	NE S1b	lever frame	50	1906
Wickenby	MS&LR	1890	MS&L3	panel		1990
Wigan Wallgate	LMSR	1941	LMS13	lever frame	75	1977
Wigton	BR(LMR)	1957	BR(LMR)15	lever frame	40	1957
Willesborough Crossing (G)	SR	nk	uSR Hut	lever frame	2	nk
Willesden	BR(LMR)	1965	BR(LMR)PB	panels		1984 & 90
Willesden Brent Sidings	LNWR	1878	LNW4	lever frame & panel	70	1906 & 84
Willesden Carriage Shed Middle (NBP)	BR(LMR)	1953	LMS11c	lever frame & panel	3	1953 & 84
Willesden Carriage Shed North	BR(LMR)	1953	LMS11c	lever frame & panel	42	1953 & 85
Willesden Carriage Shed South (NBP)	BR(LMR)	1953	LMS11c	lever frame	30	1953
Willesden High Level Junction	LMSR	1930	LNW5	panel		1985
Willesden Suburban	BR(LMR)	1988	BR(LMR)PB	panel		1988
Wilmslow	BR(LMR)	1959	BR(LMR)PB	panel		1959
Winning	NER	1895	NE N2	lever frame	15	1963

Signalbox Name	Company	Date	Design	Mechanical or Panel	No of Levers	Date of Frame or Panel
Winsford Junction	LNWR	1897	LNW4	lever frame	41	1897
Witham	BR(ER)	1961	BR(ER)18PB	panel		1961
Woburn Sands	LNWR	1904	LNW4	lever frame	25	1904
Woking	SR	1937	SR13	power frame & panels		1937 & 66
Wokingham	SR	1933	SR12	lever frame	40	1933
Wolverhampton	BR(LMR)	1965	BR(LMR)PB	panel		1965
Woodburn Junction	BR(ER)	1992	Portakabin	panel		1992
Woodgrange Park	LT&SR	1894	RSCo	lever frame	50	1894
Woodhouse East Junction	LNER	1926	LNER11a	lever frame	84	1926
Woofferton Junction	LNW&GWJt	1875E	LNW&GWJt 1	lever frame	39	1914
Wool	L&SWR	1890	LSW3b	lever frame	19	1890
Wooley Coal Siding	Railtrack	1996		panel		1996
Worcester Shrub Hill	GWR	1935	GW11	lever frame	84	1935
Workington Main No2	LNWR	1889	LNW4	lever frame	58	1889
Workington Main No3	LNWR	1886	LNW4	lever frame	25	1886
Worksop East	MS&LR	1880	MS&L2	lever frame	20	1975
Worksop West	MS&LR	1874	MS&L1	lever frame	28	1928
Wrawby Junction	GCR	1916	GC5	lever frame	137	1916
Wrenbury	LNWR	1882	LNW4	lever frame	17	1882
Wroxham	GER	1900	GE7	lever frame	50	1900
Wye	SER	1893	S&F12a	lever frame	24	1893
Wylam	NER	1897	NE N5 overhead	panel		1969
Wymondham South Junction	GER	1877	GE2	lever frame	42	nk
Yarmouth Vauxhall	GER	1884	GE4/S&F	lever frame	63	1905
Yeovil Junction	L&SWR	1909	LSW4	lever frame	44	1967
Yeovil Pen Mill	GWR	1937	GW11	lever frame	65	1937
Yoker IECC	BR(ScR)	1989	BR(ScR)PB	VDUs etc		1989
York IECC	BR(ER)	1989	BR(ER)PB	VDUs etc		1989
Ystrad Mynach South	GWR	nk	McK&H3	lever frame	45	nk

Above (157:)
Hull Paragon signalbox, opened on 23 April 1938, and photographed in December 1996. *Author*